The topic that Al and Lisa have taken on in their new book is a crucial one—*Desperate Forgiveness*. As human beings, we are all sinful and in desperate need of God's forgiveness. Then in our daily lives, His Word instructs us to "forgive as the Lord forgave [us]." Many times that can be easier to say than to put into practice, but forgiveness has an enormous impact on our relationships. My mother, Ruth Bell Graham, often said, "A good marriage consists of two good forgivers"—and she was right! The personal life stories that Al and Lisa share in this book bear witness to that truth and will help readers take a fresh look at the need for forgiveness—both extending it and receiving it—in their own lives.

FRANKLIN GRAHAM
CEO/President, Samaritan's Purse and the Billy Graham Evangelistic Association

There's only one way out of the dark hallway of bitterness, and it's through the doorway of forgiveness. Al and Lisa's new book, *Desperate Forgiveness*, is real talk for couples who have honeymoon-strong marriages and also for those who are walking through the valley of the shadow of relational death. After reading these real-life inspiring stories, you'll have the tools you need to better understand both why we forgive and how to forgive.

KIRK CAMERON

Al and Lisa Robertson are heroes for telling this wild story, warts and all. A vitally needed, transparent look at two people at their worst moments in life—and how God redeemed them and their marriage, too. We need more stories that do not shy away from how badly we are messed up and how God can shine light into our darkest moments. Read this and be encouraged.

ERIC METAXAS
New York Times bestselling author and host of the Eric Metaxas Show

In *Desperate Forgiveness*, Al and Lisa Robertson bring a powerful message of the freedom we find when we let go of past pain and hurts. Bitterness can eat us alive, but forgiveness sets us on a path of peace and redemption. If you've ever been hurt or wronged—and we all have—put *Desperate Forgiveness* at the top of your reading list today!

JASON AND DAVID BENHAM
Entrepreneurs, authors, and public speakers

As a police officer, a policy-maker, and a pastor, I've spent a lot of time dealing with issues that impact families. Among the biggest problems that fracture families are bitterness and unforgiveness. We hold on to the pain of the past and stoke the embers of anger that Christ calls us to let go. In *Desperate Forgiveness*, Al and Lisa Robertson tackle this head-on from the depth of personal experience. We all need to be reminded of the power of forgiveness. After all, it is the essence of what Jesus taught. I want to thank the Robertsons for having the courage to bring us back to the heart of the gospel.

TONY PERKINS
President, Family Research Council

We will never forget the call of desperation from Alan saying, "It's over; we can't go on." The Robertsons' marriage was at a breaking point. Should they listen to man's wisdom and end their failing marriage? Or perhaps listen to the still, small voice saying, "My grace is sufficient for you" and put back together what evil was determined to tear apart? Al and Lisa's story is a testimony to the power of God when we surrender our will. Nothing is too big and too far gone for God to heal. Come as you are and immerse yourself in their story. Then see and feel the hope that is available to you, too, when you trust in Jesus Christ.

MAC AND MARY OWEN
Celebrate Recovery national directors

Al and Lisa Robertson have a very real backstory, and they aren't afraid to talk about it. It has a lot to do with forgiveness, as all of our real stories do. In an easy-to-understand story form, Al and Lisa open us up to the many angles of the desperate forgiveness we all need to give and receive, while sharing tools to help us all. In a day when Christian leaders spend a lot of effort spinning their images, these two lay it all out, and the world is better because of it.

TIM HARLOW
Author and pastor of Parkview Christian Church

Thank you, Al and Lisa Robertson, for sharing raw honesty, biblical truth, compelling stories, and your passion for marriage in *Desperate Forgiveness*. Your life experiences and wisdom paint a true picture of the freedom and fulfillment that can emerge through forgiveness.

DAVE STONE
Pastor, Southeast Christian Church, Louisville, Kentucky

For anyone struggling with forgiveness, you'll find hope and a way forward in this book. *Desperate Forgiveness* is not the testimony of perfect people preaching Christian forgiveness. It's so much better than that. Al and Lisa, like many people, had hard and hurtful childhoods, and as adults they did their share of hurting others. This book chronicles their journey to follow the Christian imperative of forgiveness. It wasn't easy. But now their story inspires readers and shows them that no matter how bad the situation, forgiveness is possible.

ANN MCELHINNEY
Journalist, author, and filmmaker

In *Desperate Forgiveness*, my friends Al and Lisa Robertson share deeply personal stories about how the Lord led them down the path of forgiveness. With compassion and grace, they offer practical tools and guidance to help you along your own journey toward forgiveness. I truly believe this book has the potential to change the relationships in your life forever.

ROBERT MORRIS
Lead senior pastor of Gateway Church and bestselling author of *The Blessed Life, Frequency,* and *Beyond Blessed*

DESPERATE FORGIVENESS

DESPERATE FORGIVENESS

How Mercy Sets You Free

AL AND LISA ROBERTSON

With Steve and Lois Rabey

TYNDALE HOUSE PUBLISHERS, INC.
CAROL STREAM, ILLINOIS

FOCUS ON THE FAMILY® | **FOCUS ON MARRIAGE**™

We dedicate this book to those who have found themselves in a broken and desperate place, needing forgiveness from the Healer of brokenness. We pray this book helps you find your way to Him and find freedom in God's grace! If you have found His forgiveness and need to forgive someone or receive forgiveness from someone, we pray God shows you the way to release the hurt and embrace restoration whenever possible. Not all relationships can be restored on this side of heaven, but we can always be restored to our heavenly Father.

Contents

CHAPTER I

DESPERATE FOR FORGIVENESS

THERE'S AN EIGHT-YEAR-OLD BOY perched high in a magnolia tree. It's ten o'clock at night, and the evening is dark as molasses, so no one can see him—but he can see the people below just fine. He watches as his dad throws two men out the front door of the run-down juke joint, beer hall, and gambling den that his father operates for its crooked owner. The two men land in a rutted gravel parking lot, then quickly get up and begin hitting each other hard with their fists. After the one on the left knocks back the one on the right about five feet with a roundhouse punch to the cheek, the slugged man stumbles to his feet, pulls a knife out of his pants pocket, stabs the other, and runs wildly into the dark.

That was young Al Robertson up in that tree, and it was his pre–*Duck Dynasty* dad, Phil Robertson, throwing the two drunken fighters out of the joint. Phil had previously worked as a schoolteacher and coach, but he got tired of that. So he'd walked away from a decent job, determined to find a better way to make a living. That's how he wound up at a dump of a beer hall just south of El Dorado, Arkansas. The rest of the Robertson family—Al's mom, Kay, and his two younger brothers, Jase and Willie—faithfully followed along. The family of five lived in a dilapidated one-room trailer located across the parking lot from the bar.

The Robertsons were too poor to afford a TV, so young Al's nightly entertainment consisted of what happened at his father's place of employment. He saw it all: live fistfights and stabbings, prostitutes negotiating fees for their services, and wrecks of human beings who would drink until they couldn't drink anymore and then stumble outside and pass out.

A few years later, Phil would have another tired-of-that episode. This time he was sick and tired of Kay and his three boys. (Their fourth son, Jep, wasn't born yet.) Phil didn't want to see any of them anymore, so Kay took her sons to Louisiana, where she found a job.

Little Girl Lost

There's a seven-year-old girl shivering in her bed at her grandmother's house. That's where she stays when her parents go off to work each morning. Right now she's wishing with all her might that she could disappear, because she hears footsteps in the hallway and the turning of a squeaky door handle.

She knows who it is. It's a family member who will soon be touching her where she shouldn't be touched. She wants to scream out, but he warned that he would hurt her if she ever told a soul about what happens, so she shivers and tries to disappear into the bed.

That was little Lisa, who would grow up and marry Al. This hopeless scene would repeat itself over and over again for the next seven years.

Her grandmother should have known something was wrong, but she never seemed to notice. Her mother should have known something was wrong, but she was too pre-occupied with her own problems and the problems of Lisa's older, wilder sister. Overall, her mother gave little thought to the things happening in Lisa's life unless they impacted her life personally.

The older women in her life weren't there to help her, so Lisa would cry herself to sleep, blaming herself for this man's sins and dreaming that, someday, a prince would arrive to rescue her.

Two Broken People

Those two broken, abused, and neglected children married each other about a decade after these experiences, and those two people are *us*. People say that every person brings psychological and emotional baggage into marriage. We brought big, overflowing bags full of ugliness, pain, and bitterness into our relationship. We thought we could simply forget all about these bad memories and hurts, but you know how that goes. Every time we faced a minor issue or disagreement, those bags would open up and their nasty contents would pour out into our marriage.

We were two injured people, striking out blindly and hurting each other even more in an effort to overcome or ignore the things inside us that were tearing us up. The pain we inflicted on each other wasn't always intentional, but it doesn't have to be intentional to cause harm. Not only were we blind to the pain we were inflicting on each other, we were also ignorant of the one solution that could heal such hurts.

Now fast-forward a few decades.

We're older and wiser now, we're more happily married than we ever imagined possible, and we're no longer haunted by a closet full of unopened baggage. We realized that as long as we tried to ignore our brokenness and pain, it would sneak up on us in harmful ways when we weren't watching, so we went through a process of dealing with these historic hurts.

While our marriage isn't perfect, it has been miraculously transformed. Once war-torn, our union is now loving and beautiful. Our love is deeper than it has ever been, and we're grateful for the blessings of two grown children and six grandchildren (so far).

The fact that two people who couldn't even manage their own marriage are now leading marriage retreats for other couples still amazes us. We love helping the many men and women who are just as damaged, confused, and conflict-prone as we were.

Once during one of our retreats, someone asked us, "Say, how did the two of you learn about helping married people?"

We looked at each other and responded with the first thing that came to our minds: "Forgiveness!"

It's true. If it weren't for forgiveness, the two of us probably wouldn't be married to each other, not after all we've been through. We might not even be alive.

Our love story is colored with seeming opposites: brokenness and restoration, deceit and redemption, betrayal and reconciliation.

Forgiveness: What It Is and What It Isn't

Two children are playing together when one grabs the other's toy. Hopefully an adult will intervene, return the stolen toy, and restore order so the two kids can go back to playing again like nothing ever happened. That's an example of a simple form of forgiveness that many of us practice in small ways every day: letting bygones be bygones.

That's not the kind of forgiveness we're talking about in this book. We're talking about *desperate forgiveness*, the end-of-your-rope, face-in-the-dirt, empty-handed realization that you experience when you discover you cannot survive another day without giving and receiving mercy.

We're talking about the kind of desperate forgiveness people reach for and cling to when they've been completely shattered, exhausted, and drained of all pride.

We're talking about the kind of desperate forgiveness people seek when the sins they've committed in private become public, shining a bright light on dark places.

We're talking about the kind of desperate forgiveness that each and every one of us needs to reconcile our broken relationships with God and all the people in our lives: our wives, our husbands, our children, our relatives, our neighbors, our coworkers, and even our political opponents.

We're talking about the most powerful resource in the world for experiencing changed lives, revitalized marriages, rekindled relationships, and hope and healing for tomorrow.

Take a look around our world and you can see we desperately need this kind of forgiveness today. Whether you look into people's lives, or whether you look at the divisiveness and partisan anger of today's culture, you can see people torn apart by bitterness, division, and a widespread lack of forgiveness.

Thankfully, in our relationship, we reached the point of desperate forgiveness. Both of us were so desperate for our love to survive that we *had* to learn to forgive each other.

Have you ever been in that dark, desperate place where receiving forgiveness is your only answer? Or have you ever found yourself on the other side of the argument, desperately needing to offer forgiveness to another person who has hurt you?

If so, we want to invite you to accompany the two of us on a journey of forgiveness. We are glad to serve as your guides because we know the territory well. We stand before you as two desperate sinners who have experienced forgiveness through Christ and have regularly practiced offering and receiving forgiveness with each other.

Forgiveness is not only what we believe. It's how we live. In fact, we've discovered it's the only way we *can* live.

Forgive and Forget?

When you mention the word *forgiveness*, many people immediately think of commercials they've seen on TV promoting auto insurance that offers "accident forgiveness." In a sense, that's the same kind of insurance God is offering us: *life* accident forgiveness.

When others hear the word *forgiveness*, they think about a Christian teaching they may have heard. "Jesus says we should forgive each other," they say. "You know, turn the other cheek and all that."

Forgiveness is right there in the Lord's Prayer that Jesus taught His disciples to pray, and that millions of us pray every Sunday at church: "Forgive us our debts, as we also have forgiven our debtors" (Matthew 6:12).

Sounds like a simple, painless transaction. But truly forgiving someone who has hurt you is actually one of the most difficult and costly decisions a person can make. This forgiveness was won for us by Christ's sacrificial death on the cross. In fact, as Jesus was dying on that cross He prayed for God to forgive the very men and women who had persecuted and crucified Him: "Father, forgive them, for they know not what they do" (Luke 23:34).

But does forgiving mean forgetting? Does it wipe the slate clean? Not necessarily. Desperate forgiveness doesn't mean you forget the pain that others have caused you. It means you release the pain and the terrible hold it has on you so you will not be eaten up by bitterness and anger.

As the Dixie Chicks sang in their angry hit song, "Not Ready to Make Nice":

Forgive, sounds good
Forget, I'm not sure I could.[1]

Let's think back to two stories that showed the world how powerful forgiveness can be.

One morning in 2006, a man and his wife walked their two daughters to the school bus stop, then came back home. After the wife left the house, the man drove to a nearby school where he killed five young girls before killing himself. The shooting at the West Nickel Mines School, a humble one-room Amish schoolhouse in Pennsylvania's Lancaster County, outraged the nation. But the community's response may have shocked this country's people even more.

Police were still on scene investigating the tragedy when an Amish man warned his neighbors against holding bitterness against the killer. "We must not think evil of this man," he said.[2]

Within a few hours of the shooting, one Amish person visited the shooter's home to comfort his wife and children. Some later attended the killer's funeral. The Amish community even created a charitable fund for his family.

Two years later, a twenty-one-year-old white supremacist walked into an evening Bible study at Charleston's Mother Emanuel African Methodist Episcopal Church, a historic church that played a significant role in the civil rights struggles of the 1960s. He started shooting, and then he walked out of the church six minutes later, leaving nine people dead, including the senior pastor.

Within days, many from the church forgave the killer. "It took me a while," said one seventy-year-old member of the congregation. "I just felt that I've been praying 'forgive those who trespass against us' . . . for years, and now it was time to re-examine those words and practice it."[3]

The people of Nickel Mines and Charleston may never forget the pain, heartache, and tragedy of these devastating shootings, but they've chosen how they're going to respond. By forgiving cold-blooded killers, they've decided they won't be held hostage by the fear, anger, and sorrow that, over time, could eventually turn into resentment, bitterness, and a thirst for vengeance.

That's how forgiveness can heal our hurts, turn victims into victors, and transform bitterness into blessings.

Better Than the Alternatives

Forgiving others can be difficult and painful, but it's a whole lot better than the alternative. When forgiveness is refused or rejected, people can find themselves spiraling out of control, rapidly descending into darkness and depression.

Look at Judas, one of Jesus' original twelve disciples. He

was part of the inner circle. He watched Jesus forgive sinners, dine with unsavory characters, heal the broken, and tend the sick. He saw all the greatness, goodness, and grace of Jesus, but he still refused to believe that such forgiveness could be extended to him. Stuck in a whirlwind of despair, Judas was in a terrible, desperate place. His desperation revealed itself when he took his own life.

Desperation is a terrible place to wind up. Today, many people walk through life caught in the same kind of internal storm Judas suffered. They don't experience forgiveness and become locked in bitterness. They're drowning in a spiral of shame, guilt, and fear.

Isn't that the way the devil works? He wants to close us off from God's grace, making us desperate and alone. Satan doesn't want us to relinquish our hold upon the hurt and pain that consume our existence. He wants us to ignore our emotional baggage rather than clean it out and heal our hearts.

Both of us know how sin makes people desperate—desperate to find the next thing that will alleviate the guilt, or the next relationship that will take our minds off our loneliness, or the next diversion that will give us a moment of pleasure. Some people are so desperate to find relief that they will try just about anything, as long as that relief doesn't require them to shine the light of truth upon what they know is wrong in their own lives.

Some people turn their backs on forgiveness and try to address their pain and sorrow through revenge and vengeance, like the movie heroes in *Braveheart*, *Gladiator*, or many of the early Clint Eastwood films. But no matter how many times you imagine saying, "Make my day," getting even will not heal your heart. Unforgiveness only leads to unfulfillment and loneliness.

Even so, people with closed hearts usually need to be desperate before they open themselves to God's grace. Alan witnessed this while serving as a pastor for more than twenty-five years. He knows you can't push forgiveness on someone who doesn't want it or think they need it. He tried every tool in the preacher's toolbox. He taught his people about forgiveness. He reminded them about what they were taught. He pleaded with them to act upon what he had taught them. He even tried to guilt-trip them by convicting them of their sin and their need for forgiveness. But for people with closed hearts, it typically takes real desperation before they're able to see they need forgiveness themselves.

Stories of Redemption

In this book, we'll share stories of desperate forgiveness, beginning with our own. You may know some of our story from *Duck Dynasty* or from our previous book, *A New Season*. You may know about the Robertson family. All of us have lived very public lives in recent years, and we have not been silent about our problems, our insufficiencies, our opinions, or our faith. Our family is an open book.

But there's so much more to our story. You'll learn more about our battles and victories in the pages that follow. We want to be authentic and approachable because we truly believe that when lives are changed and marriages are saved, future generations are affected. Destinies are altered through desperate forgiveness.

We'll also tell you stories about men, women, and families we know who found themselves at the end of their ropes, desperate for a way out of the darkness. These people are just like the two of us—they reached the point of desperation and then found reconciliation on the other side of forgiveness.

Amid all these stories we will share powerful biblical accounts of forgiveness both given and received. As the prophet Micah tells us, God absolutely loves forgiving us when we ask Him:

> Who is a God like you, pardoning iniquity
>   and passing over transgression
>   for the remnant of his inheritance?
> He does not retain his anger forever,
>   because he delights in steadfast love.
> He will again have compassion on us;
>   he will tread our iniquities underfoot.
> You will cast all our sins
>   into the depths of the sea.
>
> MICAH 7:18-19

Not all the stories you read in the following pages have happy endings. Some end with despair or death because the subjects closed the door on forgiveness and God's grace. Without forgiveness, desperate people tend to sink deeper into a place of despair, depression, and destruction, at least until they seek relief and restoration.

An Invitation to Healing

We pray that this book will challenge you and change your thinking about forgiveness. Perhaps you are desperate to receive forgiveness. Perhaps you desperately need to offer forgiveness to someone else. Either way, we extend you a humble invitation: Will you choose to seek a place of healing and peaceful reconciliation?

As two fallible people who have lived lives of desperation in a sinful world, we see how Satan tries to remind us every day of the many messes we made in our marriage early on. But each time he reminds us of the sins of our past, we exercise our choice and choose to not remember all the hurts, shame, and failures we've experienced. Instead, we celebrate the many healing memories and personal victories that God has brought to our lives.

As children, we lived through some evil situations. As adults, we've seen our share of sin, ugliness, and despair. But we can still tell you that there is hope. There is light. There is a way through the darkness. It begins with forgiveness. Come with us and see how forgiveness can transform your life.

CHAPTER 2

A FAMILY FORGED
BY FORGIVENESS

"WE'VE HAULED A LOT OF fish up this bank," I (Al) reminded members of my family. "We've played baseball under these trees, Si shot a few squirrels out of them as well, we all got baptized in the creek back here behind me, and now here we are," I said to my parents, "almost 50 years after you two got together, having the wedding you never had, with four generations of Robertsons looking on. I'd say this is the perfect spot."[1]

If you're going to make your national television debut, you might as well make it big! At least that was how it happened for me when I joined my family to launch the fourth season of the megapopular *Duck Dynasty* TV series.

Somehow my family had achieved fame without me. While they were becoming reality TV stars, I—the so-called "Beardless Brother"—was busy pastoring a church. Now that the show was to feature my parents' marriage vow–renewal ceremony, the call went out for the oldest (and I would add, wisest and best-looking) brother. "Let's get Pastor Alan."

If I wanted to twist the truth a bit, I could claim my big debut kicked the show into a whole new gear. After all, the "Till Duck Do Us Part" episode attracted 11.8 million viewers, making it the most popular episode of the series and the highest rated telecast in A&E's history as a network. But I know better. It wasn't me that drew the big response. It was love.

Everybody has their own definition of love, but the emotions seen on the show that night were a testimony to the kind of love that's forgiving, life changing, and hard won, exactly the kind of Christian love Paul described in his famous "love chapter":

> Love is patient and kind; love does not envy or boast;
> it is not arrogant or rude. It does not insist on its
> own way; it is not irritable or resentful; it does not
> rejoice at wrongdoing, but rejoices with the truth.
> Love bears all things, believes all things, hopes all
> things, endures all things.
>
> 1 CORINTHIANS 13:4-7

This was the love our family saw that day when Phil and Kay finally got to enjoy the kind of beautiful wedding ceremony they'd missed out on when they married as poor teenagers nearly fifty years earlier. The simple vows they shared on the program spoke of a love that had seen its share of ups and downs.

"From the time I was fourteen years old, I loved you," said Kay, who wore a lovely white dress. "I loved you when we were poor and you were not so nice. Now you're really nice and kind, and I'm not going anywhere. I will love you forever."

You could tell Phil respected the ceremony's importance. It was so important that he temporarily traded in his standard uniform of camouflage clothing for a snazzy blue blazer.

"You have cooked me many a good meal," he said. "From your loins came four healthy, godly men. You are my best friend, I love you dearly, and I'm going to be with you for the long haul, till they put me in the ground."[2]

It was a moving ceremony. Jase even cried a bit. But deep down all of us knew one thing: This family was different before God's grace came into our home. We realized:

There never would have been a Phil and Kay . . .

There never would have been a marriage vow–renewal ceremony . . .

There never would have been a popular TV show featuring our family . . .

And you probably never would have heard of a company called Duck Commander . . . if it weren't for the radical, reconciling power of forgiveness. Without forgiveness, none of these beautiful things would have happened.

"No Record of Wrongs"

It was fun being on TV with my family for this amazing event. Afterward I enjoyed reading reviews and articles that tried to explain why this episode had been so popular. My favorite article appeared in the magazine *National Review*, which typically focuses on politics and current events.

This article explained the numerical significance of our achievement in attracting nearly twelve million viewers by comparing our audience to the audiences of popular shows: "It's also 8 million more viewers than the season-five premiere of *Mad Men*. It's nearly 6 million more than this year's premiere of *Breaking Bad*. And it's almost 3 million more than the finale of *The Good Wife*."[3]

Not surprisingly, the article did not cite my big debut as the primary reason for the show's success, instead focusing on the important role faith plays in the lives of the members of the Robertson clan: "It shows Christian men and women living ordinary lives that are informed by their faith —informed by their commitment to God, and each other. These are not the dour, joyless Christians you so often see on the screen, and too often run into in life. They don't go around quoting Scripture or heaping judgment on others; they're too busy having fun and living good lives."[4]

I say "Amen!" to that. The main reason we Robertsons don't judge each other for our many flaws and failures is because all of us have experienced the life-changing power of desperate forgiveness. It takes forgiveness for all of us to live out the kind of Christian love Paul described. Our love for each other "is not easily angered" (1 Corinthians 13:5, NIV), even though there's plenty to get angry about if you want to be angry. Our love for each other is a love that "keeps no record of wrongs" (1 Corinthians 13:5, NIV), even though there have been plenty of wrongs to record, if you like counting other people's sins.

Forgiveness is at the heart of our family dynamic, and like I said, there wouldn't even be a Robertson family to talk about if it wasn't for the kind of desperate forgiveness that led a frightened and heartbroken Kay to give one more chance to Phil, her angry, sometimes abusive husband who, during one of his drunken rages, told her and the three of us kids to get out of his life.

Darkness to Light

When that happened, we left as quickly as we could. The four of us were entering some of the darkest times during Dad's "rompin' stompin' days." I was nine years old. I didn't know if I would ever see him again. I had no idea what the rest of us were going to do.

We spent a night at an uncle's house before some nice people at White's Ferry Road Church in West Monroe, Louisiana, embraced our broken family and helped us find a low-rent apartment where we could stay. (You will be hearing more about this so-called "Duck Dynasty Church" in the pages to come. It's not only the church that wrapped its loving arms around our family when we were desperate, it's the church where I served as pastor for twenty-five years, and it's where Lisa and I first taught these lessons on forgiveness.)

The four of us did what we could to make the best of a bad situation. My mom got a good job while I took care of my two younger brothers, Jase and Willie. By the time I was ten years old, I had become an expert at changing diapers, preparing bottles, and cooking up fried bologna sandwiches for the little ones under my care. I grew up fast during those years because Mom needed me to be strong.

It was during this desperate time that we started going to church at White's Ferry Road. My awareness and love for God grew rapidly as I attended church on Sundays and as members picked me up for Bible studies on other days of the week. I also loved riding on the church's pink buses with other kids to church events. Having grown up with an unstable, no-good, drunken father like mine, I was deeply attracted to the steadfast love of my heavenly Father.

One night when Miss Kay had been doubting her ability to take care of us like we needed, I said something to her out of the blue. "God will take care of us, Mom." The words just came out. I hadn't planned on saying them. Later on, I would think of this as my very first sermon! It's certainly my shortest sermon, and it's a sign that the four of us had opened up a door for God's light to shine into our dark and depressing circumstances.

Because Phil had a bad temper, Kay warned her coworkers to be prepared if he ever showed up at the office seeking her out, telling them they might need to call 911 if he was really upset. Finally, one day he did show up. A coworker told Kay he was sitting in his truck in the company parking lot.

Kay was expecting the worst as she approached, and sure enough, she could see him slumped over the steering wheel. *Drunk as a skunk again!* she told herself. But upon closer inspection, things were far different than they first appeared.

Phil saw her and raised his head. She could see he was crying.

"I want my family back," he told her. "I'm so sorry."

Phil was clearly desperate for forgiveness. The man who had angrily walked out on her and her children was now begging her for one more chance. Perhaps you can put yourself in her shoes. Perhaps you can picture her weighing her options as she sought what was best for the five people involved.

Would she find it in her heart to overlook the years of anger and drunkenness, dishonesty, and insensitivity? Would it even be right for her to forgive a man who had made a mess of his own life as well as her life and ours?

The fate of our family hung in the balance as Kay quickly considered her response. She answered with an amazing blend of love and wisdom. She agreed to welcome back the man she loved, the man who had hurt her and her three boys so many times. But she didn't do so blindly. She stipulated some important conditions.

"Well, Phil," she said, "the boys want you back. I want you back. We love you, but we can't do it the way we were doing it. We can't take you like you are."

"I want to change," he said, "but I don't know how."

"Well, I know a guy who can help you."

The guy she was talking about was the pastor at White's Ferry Road. He had tried talking to Dad back when he was running the bar, but Dad had thrown him out and told him not to come back. Phil dismissed him as a "Bible thumper" and "holy roller."

Miss Kay laid out the conditions Phil would be required to follow. Not only would Phil talk to the pastor and listen to his sermons on Sundays, but he would also need to forsake his old drinking buddies and say farewell to all rompin' and stompin'.

Phil was so desperate to have his family back that he readily agreed to all her conditions. After a hurried family reunion, Phil spent the next three nights talking to our pastor and studying the Bible before he finally relented and gave his life to God.

We were amazed to witness his sudden interior transformation in the coming days and weeks. Phil's entire direction in life began to change. Instead of dismissing God and those who preached the Bible, he turned into a big sponge, soaking up every drop of biblical wisdom he could get by attending church on Sunday mornings and other times during the week and participating in Bible studies every night. He was baptized at the age of twenty-eight.

The life change I saw in Dad inspired me and showed me how God can do powerful miracles in even the most unlikely people's lives. Phil seemed like a different person from the unpleasant and undependable man we had known for so

long. Almost overnight, he went from being the worst rep-
robate in the area to leading people to Christ like crazy. He
went from being a jerk to being a John-the-Baptist type—
and Phil actually looks like what John the Baptist would have
looked like, I think, aside from the sunglasses and camouflage clothing.

It was a dramatic conversion that reminded me of the
conversion of the apostle Paul. Before he was a Christian,
he was a Pharisee known as Saul who ruthlessly persecuted
early Christians. One day, as he was on his way to harass
some more believers, he had a surprising encounter with
the resurrected Christ. A bright light from heaven blinded
Saul, who fell to the ground. Over the next few days, Paul
accepted Christ's will for his life, becoming an evangelist
who preached Christ's gospel near and far.

Phil wasn't like Paul. He hadn't persecuted Christians; he
merely made fun of them and dismissed their beliefs. But
his conversion changed everything. A man who had turned
his back on God had been personally touched by the power
of Christ's forgiveness. Phil quickly turned into a kind of
apostle Paul himself, preaching and teaching God's Word
anytime anyone would listen.

We're all grateful things turned out this way, and we all
realize none of this would have happened without desperate
forgiveness.

Without this desperate forgiveness, there wouldn't have
been four generations of Robertsons celebrating Phil and
Kay's vow ceremony.

Without this desperate forgiveness, there wouldn't be any Duck Commander, the company Phil founded. For years our family members were the company's sole employees (or slave laborers). The company originally operated out of Phil and Kay's house, and Miss Kay served us lunch every day.

Without this desperate forgiveness, there wouldn't be any *Duck Dynasty* show to entertain and inspire so many people. If our family hadn't been turned around and directed toward God, we would have remained broken, angry people. Who would ever want to see a TV show about that?

I am a child of forgiveness. When everything in my life was totally screwed up, God changed it all through the power of His grace. After Miss Kay found it in her heart to forgive Phil, the rest of us did too.

My experience with forgiveness throughout my life is the main reason I'm writing this book with Lisa. Both of us have encountered the life-changing reality of God's loving mercy.

We want you to experience the same forgiveness amidst the complicated relationships in your own life. We want you to see all the good things that are possible for you on the other side of desperate forgiveness.

Giving It All Up

You might think that after our family's spiritual rebirth I would stay on a godly path until the time I became a pastor— but you would be wrong. As great as it is for me to talk about how Phil's problem led him to a new relationship with God, it's time I own up to some of my own needs for desperate forgiveness.

With the new-and-improved Phil back in our lives, our family was happier than we had ever been. Mom and Dad were new Christians who regularly took all of us to church. But at the same time, I could sense a darkness growing in me. It almost seemed that after the devil lost some of his prime territory in Phil's soul, he turned his attention to me, the next-weakest link in the family.

My sins were the typical ones. I started to slide into drinking, drugs, and sex. Most of the time I hid it well. I was a great deceiver. Sure, people could tell something was wrong, but Mom and Dad seemed to deny what they could plainly see with their own eyes. But after I graduated from high school, I became less cautious about covering my tracks. I figured, *Hey, I'm an adult now.* That's when Phil grabbed me and sat me down for a long talk.

"Al," he said, "you shouldn't be living like this."

The irony of the situation amazed me. The former drunk who abandoned our family was now counseling me on godly behavior. I didn't like it one bit.

"If you are going to keep on living your life the way you've been living it, you can't stay here and influence your brothers," he told me. "Either you've got to change, or you've got to hit the road."

I was shocked I was getting kicked out of my own family, and the timing could not have been worse. I had just started a relationship with a beautiful girl named Lisa who I had known for years. But now I would be leaving home. I promised Lisa I would remain faithful to her and suggested we have a long-distance relationship. This was a lie, as I had no intention of avoiding other women.

I was seventeen years old and desperately trying to find myself. Looking back at the whole situation now, I can see that all I found was trouble. But at the time I was enticed by the temptations of the big city. I was on my way to New Orleans.

My Prodigal Period

A tire iron is a wonderful tool for changing a tire, but it's a painful tool when grabbed by a violent man who uses it to repeatedly hit you. That sudden realization explains why I was literally running for my life from a man who had good reasons for wanting to kill me.

God works in mysterious ways. In my case, He used a weaponized tire iron as a powerful tool to bring me to my senses and back to Him after a yearlong period as a prodigal son.

I had moved to LaPlace, Louisiana, a suburb of New Orleans, where I lived with my aunt and got a night job at the local hospital in nearby Kenner. I still wanted some kind of connection to family, but not too much. Mostly, I was out doing my own thing without any adult supervision. One thing led to another, and I was soon drinking all day and then doing drugs with my nighttime coworkers.

I also started a relationship with a nurse who worked at the hospital. I realized this was a violation of everything I had promised Lisa, but I didn't care. I was eighteen by that point and felt like this was my time to live. The nurse was twenty-six and married. As I understood things, she had been separated from her husband for many months, but as I would very soon realize, they had only been apart for a couple of weeks when I arrived on the scene, and tempers were hot.

One Sunday after I had been with my nurse girlfriend at her apartment, I left to go back to my place. But as I headed for my car, I was surprised to see that it had two flat tires. I had seen plenty of flats in my life, but never two at a time. I didn't give it any further thought and got to work removing one of the tires.

That's when I heard someone coming up behind me, yelling and cursing. As I turned, I saw a man grab the tire iron I had just been using. The next thing I knew, he was hitting me with it. After taking a few blows, I wrestled with him a bit. When that didn't slow him down, I took off running. Thankfully I was faster than my attacker, who followed behind, carrying a gun.

I dashed into a nearby 7-Eleven and yelled at the clerk, "Some jerk is attacking me! Call 911 now!" My adrenaline flowing, I looked for any handy item I could use to ward off my attacker should he reappear. That's how I came to be standing crouched inside that convenience store holding tightly to my unlikely weapon of self-defense—a toilet plunger—when the cops drove by.

I headed back toward my car and encountered a scene that looked like it came from *CSI* or some other TV cop show. My attacker was sitting in the back of the police car explaining his actions. My girlfriend, who had come down to survey the chaos, took turns yelling at her husband and at me. My car was covered in dents from the tire iron, which my attacker had used to break my windshield and gouge deep holes in my dashboard.

Two policemen looked at me with disgust. They saw little more than a punk, an eighteen-year-old kid who was sleeping with a guy's wife. It turns out the man who attacked me was actually a drug informant working for the police force, so he was one of their own.

There's no law against being a punk who sleeps with another man's wife, so the police didn't arrest me. Eventually, the police cars drove off. My assailant and his wife had left too. It was just me and my ridiculous car, which, in addition to its two flat tires, now sported so many dings and dents that it looked like it had been through one of the world's worst hailstorms.

I sat down on the curb and started crying. Suddenly, I could see how pitiful my little life was. I thought I was a big man making his way in the world, but I was just a lost boy making a mess of things. If there had been somebody nearby to cry out to, I would have begged for some kind of help.

That's when I heard a click and noticed someone was still there. A crime scene photographer was snapping pictures of the area. Now this camera-toting cop was zeroing in on my beat-up car. I didn't realize it yet, but this man was about to become my guardian angel.

"Where are you from, kid?" he asked me in a warm,

friendly tone that contrasted with the icy response I'd received from the other officers.

When I told him I was from West Monroe, he asked me another question.

"So, what's going on back home right now?"

I asked him for some assistance so I could answer his question. "Can you tell me what day it is?"

"It's Sunday," he said.

"What time is it?"

"It's about twelve thirty."

Suddenly I could picture a beautiful scene in my mind. "Well, if it's Sunday at twelve thirty, my family is probably sitting around the dinner table. They just got home from church, and they're probably talking about the sermon, discussing what they learned, and joking about who said what to whom all morning." Describing the scene brought even more tears to my eyes. *That's where I need to be right now!* I thought.

That's the moment I made a momentous decision. I couldn't keep living this way. It was time for me to go home. If I didn't go now, I might never live to see my nineteenth birthday. It had taken a while, but I had finally come to my senses. Just like the Prodigal Son in the fifteenth chapter of Luke, I went back home to be with my family. Unlike the Prodigal Son, I first had to stop at a service station to fix two flat tires.

Somehow in my excitement, I never stopped to thank that humble police officer who had become my angel. I can't wait to get to heaven to find him and thank him for helping me more than he will ever know. And whenever I can, I thank officers for their hard work and the powerful, positive roles they can play in people's lives.

Receiving Forgiveness Is Easier Than Giving It

I turned my back on my prodigal period and was warmly welcomed back into the Robertson fold. I confessed my sins to God and begged for His forgiveness. I went on with my life.

But while forgiveness relieved my guilt, it did not erase the consequences of my sinful actions. A murderer can seek forgiveness, but the person he killed remains dead. I hadn't killed anyone, but I had stabbed Lisa in the back through my dishonesty and unfaithfulness to her. My actions had consequences not only in my life but also in hers. I had broken her heart and injured her spirit. She would find her own ways to deal with these hurts by reaching out to other men.

Years later, we would marry each other, but we could not immediately erase the stains of these early problems. In time, I would face a situation where the roles were reversed. Could I forgive Lisa for her sins against me?

Forgiveness seemed impossible for me to offer once the shoe was on the other foot. I will let Lisa tell this story in the next chapter.

CHAPTER 3

THE WOMAN
AT THE WELL

"I KNOW WHAT'S GOING ON, AND I want you to tell me about it," Al said to me one evening after a day of unusual quiet for him. We were in the kitchen, and our girls were asleep in their bedrooms.

I'd had no idea what was wrong, but his words now left no doubt in my mind that he knew something about the affair I'd been having with an old boyfriend for more than a year.

Ten years earlier, I had engaged in an emotional affair featuring plenty of fantasy but no sex. That fling almost ruined our marriage. We survived that storm, but Al had warned me then, "If you ever do anything like this again, I will divorce you!"

This time, I had not only given in to an emotional affair but had become entangled in a sexual affair as well. I had tried to hide it all but had failed. Now Al was demanding answers about this terrible mistake I'd made. My heart was racing, and sweat beads were rolling down my face. I was so scared. I just wanted to run. Al told me he needed the truth, but I denied any immoral relationship. He kept insisting I tell him the truth!

"If I tell you the truth, you're not going love me—you're going to leave me!" I cried out in a frightened admission of guilt.

"If you don't tell me the truth, I'll leave anyway!" he answered.

At that moment a startling change happened deep inside of me. I didn't hear an audible voice, but I was aware of some kind of presence that silently spoke these words to me: *I'm here. If you just tell the truth, I'll take care of it.*

I had long believed in Jesus, and I had been baptized ages earlier. But my sinful, duplicitous behavior showed I wasn't making choices like someone who lived out Christian values in her own life. The experience of actually feeling God's presence inside me was something totally new. The whole episode startled me, but at the same time this interior presence gave me the courage I needed to finally be honest.

"Okay," I said, turning to Al. "It's all true."

The Inquisition
Al questioned me throughout the night and well into the morning. I answered all his questions truthfully, even though it

was incredibly painful to do so. I had no illusions. I knew I had done some things that Al would probably find unforgivable. That was understandable based on my past behavior.

Al and I wrote about the affair and its aftermath in our book *A New Season*, so I won't repeat the whole account here. But as he interrogated me that evening, four things became crystal clear:

1. I had sinned against Al by repeatedly cheating on him.

2. I had sinned against Al's family as I worked for their company, by taking money from Duck Commander to support a double life.

3. I had tried to cover my tracks by opening up a new credit card account in my father's name to support my cheating lifestyle.

4. Most of all, I had sinned against God.

I possessed just enough courage to bare my soul and tell Al everything. From the moment I sensed God's presence with me, the walls of protection I'd carefully constructed out of lies and denial came crashing down.

After hours of Al's relentless questioning, I was devastated to see the person I had become. My awareness of that inner voice of God began to fade away and doubts grew inside of me. Maybe God was not going to take care of me after all. I cried and struggled to put words to the awful reality of my betrayal of my marriage, often making lame excuses for what I'd done in order to minimize the severe breach of trust I'd caused between Al and me.

When the interrogation was over, Al told me to move out of the house and get away from him. "And you won't be taking the girls with you!" he added.

Al's words sounded like a judge's life sentence. Where was my God now?

Weakened by hours of difficult discussion, I staggered out into our backyard and fell facedown on the ground. Feelings of loneliness and desperation pinned me to that spot in the dirt. I had nothing left. I felt worthless, shameful, dirty, and exhausted. I knew I could not go on any longer carrying all the guilt that was piling up.

A Ray of Light

Darkness seemed to completely surround me. But as I opened my eyes, a sliver of light pierced my despair. The back-porch light was still on. That bright beam in the midst of the evening's blackness stirred something deep inside me. The same divine presence I'd felt as I told Al the truth now broke through my utter desolation. I pushed myself up to a sitting position and started talking to God.

"I'm not even sure You are real," I told Him. "I thought I had a relationship with You, but right now I don't even know if You exist. If You do, would You please come and rescue me?"

Immediately it seemed like a two-ton weight was lifted off of me. I felt like God was bending down to pick me up and rescue me from the ash heap of guilt and shame where I found myself. I felt His living presence in a powerful way.

I had walked out of the house some time earlier feeling totally alone and desperate. But I felt different when I struggled back to my feet and walked back into the house. I had no idea what would happen with Al and me, but I knew what was going to happen with God and me. Both my love for Jesus and my commitment to Him were firm. I believed deeply in my soul that He would be with me, no matter what happened.

I did move out of the house and in with a friend. The girls did stay with Al. But Al did not divorce me as he had warned. I didn't realize it at the time, but Al was wrestling with what he should do. He still loved me, but could he ever trust me again? He knew God had forgiven him for many sins, but could he now forgive me for my sins against him and our marriage?

After some time, Al responded to me much the same way Miss Kay had responded to Phil: with forgiveness and conditions. For me the conditions were brutal but worthwhile. I gave Al complete access to my cell phone, e-mail, and social media accounts so he could monitor what I was communicating and with whom. I confessed my sins to his entire family and wrote a letter asking for their forgiveness, and later I confessed those same sins to the entire congregation at White's Ferry Road, where Al was the pastor.

Today we have been reconciled for twenty years and our love is stronger than ever—together. And even though I regret the pain I caused in our marriage, I'm grateful for that soul-changing encounter I had with Jesus in my backyard. Somehow my own sin and depravity drove me closer to Jesus than I had ever been before. My own life is now a testimony to desperate forgiveness.

The story of my adultery and deception shocked Al's family and the members of our church. I wouldn't be surprised if it shocks you, too. Many people told Al that I had gone too far and he should never forgive me.

"She's damaged goods," one trusted friend told him.

But my behavior didn't shock Jesus. He knew all about the brokenness and the sinful desires deep inside of me. I knew this because of the amazing encounter Jesus had with a woman much like me. Let's take a fresh look at John 4:4-30, because this woman's story is my story.

High Noon on the Wrong Side of Town

She walked through the heat of the day with an earthen water pot tucked under one arm. Her eyes were downcast so she wouldn't need to look away if some other person was silly enough to venture out into the heat at this time of day.

The people in town knew her story—how she'd been through five marriages and was now with a man who wasn't even her husband. They cast dark glances her way and avoided talking with her. Today, just like every other day, she'd made the tedious walk with the heavy pot to fetch fresh water at noontime, when it was too hot for others to be out and she could avoid their ostracism.

This was a seemingly normal day, just like all the rest—until it wasn't. Here's how the Bible describes it:

> Now when Jesus learned that the Pharisees had heard that Jesus was making and baptizing more disciples than John (although Jesus himself did not baptize, but only his disciples), he left Judea and departed again for Galilee. And he had to pass through Samaria. So he came to a town of Samaria called Sychar, near the field that Jacob had given to his son Joseph. Jacob's well was there; so Jesus, wearied as he was from his journey, was sitting beside the well. It was about the sixth hour.
>
> JOHN 4:1-6

Jesus and the disciples had been walking north for some time on their way to Galilee. Some travelers might have lengthened their journey and gone around Samaria to avoid even being in the proximity of this notorious hotbed of various religious cults and ethnic cultures. Although Samaria was part of Israel, altars to Baal and sites of pagan worship of other false gods remained. Righteous Jews were not to be seen near lowly Samaritans.

Jesus wasn't hindered by such concerns and took the more direct route. By noon He and His disciples had arrived in Samaria. It was blisteringly hot, and Jesus was thirsty.

A woman from Samaria came to draw water. Jesus
said to her, "Give me a drink." (For his disciples
had gone away into the city to buy food.) The
Samaritan woman said to him, "How is it that
you, a Jew, ask for a drink from me, a woman
of Samaria?" (For Jews have no dealings with
Samaritans.)

JOHN 4:7-9

A Controversial Personal Encounter

Jesus was there by Himself when the Samaritan woman came
to the well. If the disciples had still been with Jesus, she might
have turned away to avoid the crowd. No Jewish man would
want to be seen with a Samaritan woman—particularly *this*
woman.

The woman, hot and tired as she approached the well
with eyes downcast, probably hadn't even seen the Jewish
man sitting nearby.

"Will you give me a drink?" He asked.

She nearly dropped her water pot at the sound of His voice.
Who was this talking directly to her in this way? She could
see that Jesus was a Jew, so their being together was not only
a religious and cultural problem but one of propriety as well.

Jesus answered her, "If you knew the gift of God,
and who it is that is saying to you, 'Give me a drink,'
you would have asked him, and he would have given
you living water." The woman said to him, "Sir, you

have nothing to draw water with, and the well is
deep. Where do you get that living water? Are you
greater than our father Jacob? He gave us the well
and drank from it himself, as did his sons and his
livestock."

JOHN 4:10-12

She didn't understand what He meant about some
special kind of water. He had no water pot to lower into
the well. Was this man suffering from heatstroke? Did He
think He was greater than her famous ancestor? Did this
man saying these things not know about her unsavory
reputation?

Jesus said to her, "Everyone who drinks of this
water will be thirsty again, but whoever drinks of
the water that I will give him will never be thirsty
again. The water that I will give him will become in
him a spring of water welling up to eternal life." The
woman said to him, "Sir, give me this water, so that
I will not be thirsty or have to come here to draw
water."

JOHN 4:13-15

She accepted Jesus' offer but still didn't comprehend His
meaning. She wanted to have the special water He offered so
she wouldn't have to keep coming back to the well every day
at noon to draw water.

Getting Personal

That's when the conversation took an interesting turn.

> Jesus said to her, "Go, call your husband, and
> come here." The woman answered him, "I have no
> husband." Jesus said to her, "You are right in saying,
> 'I have no husband'; for you have had five husbands,
> and the one you have now is not your husband.
> What you have said is true."
>
> JOHN 4:16-18

Jesus apparently wanted this needy woman to realize who He really was. Using a question He knew the answer to, He exposed the way she was currently living and her alarming past. This story doesn't tell us why she had been married so many times, but the point this revelation makes clear is that Jesus, a stranger she had never seen before, knew the most intimate details about her life.

He looked like a tired traveler, not some con man promoting mind reading. Looking more closely, she recognized something authentic in Him.

> The woman said to him, "Sir, I perceive that you are
> a prophet. Our fathers worshiped on this mountain,
> but you say that in Jerusalem is the place where
> people ought to worship." Jesus said to her, "Woman,
> believe me, the hour is coming when neither on
> this mountain nor in Jerusalem will you worship

the Father. You worship what you do not know; we worship what we know, for salvation is from the Jews. But the hour is coming, and is now here, when the true worshipers will worship the Father in spirit and truth, for the Father is seeking such people to worship him. God is spirit, and those who worship him must worship in spirit and truth." The woman said to him, "I know that Messiah is coming (he who is called Christ). When he comes, he will tell us all things." Jesus said to her, "I who speak to you am he."

JOHN 4:19-26

What could a prophet, much less the Messiah, be doing here in this land where she and the other Samaritan Jews now lived? They were descendants of Israel's early leaders, but they had been told that they could only worship in Jerusalem. Meanwhile, other religions had taken over parts of the country, building altars to their gods. Confusion about how and where to worship led to many Jews bowing before false gods.

Would this man now explain everything? Would He show her how she could worship in Spirit and truth?

Just then his disciples came back. They marveled that he was talking with a woman, but no one said, "What do you seek?" or, "Why are you talking with her?" So the woman left her water jar and went away into town and said to the people, "Come, see a man who told

me all that I ever did. Can this be the Christ?" They
went out of the town and were coming to him.

JOHN 4:27-30

A Life-Changing Encounter

Suddenly, the woman's spiritual eyes were opened! She didn't
even hear the grumblings of the disciples. She grasped who
Jesus was and what that meant to her. He was the long-
awaited Messiah. His Spirit had touched her heart. A deep
need was met in her that she hadn't even known existed. The
hopes of her ancestors were restored in her as she ran off to
town to tell others about the Messiah.

She'd forgotten about drawing water from the well or the
need to get out of the noonday sun! Looking into Jesus' eyes,
she'd felt His total acceptance and embrace, despite her sinful
life. He knew what she'd done without being told. Yet He
offered living water that transformed her life. The water He
offered met the needs of her damaged soul.

We don't know what happened to this woman after this
unusual encounter. We do know by her actions that Jesus
revealed Himself to her. She was transformed from a shamed
sinner into a joyful bearer of wonderful news. She wasn't
hiding anymore. She had received living water that would
change her life for the better, and she was telling her world
about it.

I Am Standing with Her

Some Bible characters are hard for me to picture, but I can totally relate to that Samaritan woman at the well. My life was a mess. Jesus knew that when He spoke to me as I lay on the ground in my backyard after confessing my sins to Al. Before I saw that beam of the porch light, I thought that any good thing in my life was now gone. Al would divorce me. He'd take our girls away. His family, who had become my family, would disassociate from me. My friends would desert me. I would have nothing to live for.

Then, Jesus revealed Himself to me. I'd tasted the revelation of His impact in my life before, but this was different. Like the woman at the well, I was in front of Him in all my brokenness. I wasn't carrying a water pot. I was crying my eyes out on the ground in the backyard of our home at the age of thirty-five. I'd admitted the terrible guilt I carried. I'd cried out to Him in desperation. He accepted me and picked me up out of the dirt, and then He pointed my feet in the direction of the kitchen. I went in and began the journey of restoration.

I would like to think that's what happened to the Samaritan woman. Having been touched by the Master's mercy myself, I can't imagine her turning her back on the glorious opportunity to live a new life. When God's forgiveness is received and accepted, it is life changing!

Reliving the Sins of the Past

My past may be shocking to some, just as shocking as that Samaritan woman's past. But prior to Jesus turning my life around, it seems I kept repeating my past over and over again.

I am not the typical pastor's wife. My upbringing may not be anything like yours. But like that Samaritan woman at the well, I've had my life filled to overflowing with Christ's living water. I hope you can tap into and experience the flood of God's forgiveness. I have been released from the stranglehold my past once had on me. You can be free too.

My past had a huge impact on the way I lived my life. I was a promiscuous young woman, having sex with boys I dated. I've experienced the sad consequences of my chosen lifestyle (see chapter 5). Unknowingly, I carried all these unexamined sins of my past into my marriage with Al. Like a horror-movie swamp creature you just can't kill off, my recurring sins kept coming back, expressing themselves through the emotional and sexual affairs I sought out.

Why did I do those things? That's the question I asked myself a million times. Why was I "loose" with guys, even though I had been told girls like that would get a bad reputation? In my world, being loose meant that guys liked you, liked to take you out, and told you lots of nice things about how cute you were and how much of a good time you were. I didn't realize this was the way I operated at the time, in part because I was in denial. I was closing my eyes to the truth and believing lies.

Everything changed when I married Al—at least it

changed for a long time. I had married the man of my dreams, we had two beautiful girls, he was a pastor, and we were a part of a godly family.

It's that incessant question again. Why did I do those things? How had I fallen so badly after so many years of being faithful in my marriage?

One reason became clear as I spent more time processing my experiences. With the help of a Christian counselor, I came to see that I had never fully dealt with the sexual abuse I suffered as a child. Understandably, I had tried to bury it or ignore this part of my past. But no matter how deep I buried it, it never went away. It stayed there inside, continuing to cause new damage in my life. The pattern of lying, hiding my pain, and not admitting what was going on in my childhood years had built a facade that hid the real me.

Why Don't We Do What We Want to Do?

I'm not claiming that the years of sexual abuse offer an excuse for my freely chosen teenage and adult behavior. I'm saying these painful experiences planted seeds of self-doubt, dishonesty, and secrecy deep in my heart. Over time, I came to believe a lie: my purpose on this earth is to please men.

I know a number of people don't put much stock in digging up their painful pasts. They think, *What's the point? Yes, some terrible things happened to me then, but nothing can be done about that now! Just pray and move on.*

I'm no psychologist, but I've seen amazing things happen when God uses trained psychologists and counselors to help broken, sinful people understand why we do what we do. The apostle Paul would have made a great counselor because he understood how sin stains human behavior: "For I do not understand my own actions," Paul wrote. "For I do not do what I want, but I do the very thing I hate" (Romans 7:15). Paul went on to explain that we have two natures in us that struggle with each other: a sinful nature and a nature controlled by the Spirit.

Each one of us has these two competing natures, but when we're blind to this internal dynamic we may wind up doing things we don't really want to do. Looking at our pasts can help remove our blinders, letting us see the legacy of sin in people's lives and across generations. It shines a light on the lies that Satan has used to control us and direct us to a dangerous and sinful path.

In my case, *someone else's* sinful nature resulted in harm being done to me. Then *my own* sinful nature resulted in me causing harm to Alan, the only man I've ever loved.

Child abuse is a sin that breaks children into pieces. In 2014, Child Protection Service agencies in the US received an estimated 3.6 million referrals involving about 6.6 million children.[1] The abuse may be sexual, physical, verbal, emotional, or spiritual. All damage the hearts and minds of little children.

As a child, I coped with abuse by believing lies and making decisions based on them. The benefit of counseling is clear: If we can expose the lies and know the truth, then the sin someone used against us as children no longer has the power to overrule God's truth. We can break the hold that sin has on our minds and hearts through the power of the Holy Spirit.

Into My Secret World

Today I can speak openly about the secrets I once guarded so closely. Here's how the sin of sexual abuse overruled the Spirit's truth in my life, at least until I had to face facts when I was thirty-five and crying in my backyard.

When I was growing up, a family member began molesting me when I was seven years old. He never had intercourse with me, but he repeatedly engaged in sexual activities with me that badly damaged my thinking. The abuse went on until I was fourteen.

That was when I finally stood up for myself and told him: "If you ever touch me again, I'll tell my dad. And *he will kill you!*" The abuse stopped.

Until that moment I had kept everything secret. The man who abused me told me he would tell my dad if I ever said anything about it. I adored my dad, and the abuse made me feel so dirty that I didn't want him—or anyone—to know I'd ever been touched that way. Like many children, I thought the abuse was my fault. Somehow I believed the lie that my daddy would hate me for being a bad girl. I felt powerless to change what was happening because my abuser was a big, strong grown-up. I thought if I could just keep it a secret, my daddy would still love me.

This vicious cycle of secrecy and lies took root deep within me. The abuser's sinful nature had won the battle inside of him. Now his abusive behavior toward me resulted in a lie taking up residence in me, twisting my desires and leading me to make poor choices as I grew older.

Eager to Please

As a teenager, I believed my purpose was to please boys. Instead of being a wallflower, I was noticed. My low self-esteem was boosted by the compliments that usually preceded sex. I believed I was a worthwhile person if a boy wanted to have sex with me.

I thought marriage would change everything, but my two natures continued to war within me. Superficially, Al and I were doing well. Our lives were busy and seemingly successful. As the preacher's wife, I was an important part of the church. I heard every sermon and went to every women's class. I even helped Al write some of his sermons during his years in preaching school. I knew right and wrong, but my problem was that I didn't know my own soul.

Al and I were fulfilling our roles of pastor and pastor's wife, but we took each other for granted. He was busy with the church, and I was busy with my duties. Though I experienced feelings of low self-esteem creeping into my thinking, I just kept going while pushing down the reality of the darkness taking over more and more of my heart.

Not surprisingly, over time Al and I grew apart. Satan took up residence in my mind without me even knowing it. Doubts about myself crept into my thinking. I knew that I had never really considered myself worthy of Al. I had married my Prince Charming, but I wasn't good enough for him. The lies that had entered my mind when I was a little girl began to overtake me as an adult.

Just when my situation was most precarious, I crossed paths with an ex-boyfriend and sparks ignited inside me. Maybe this man could help my damaged self-esteem. The longer I toyed with this idea, the more my desires grew. I thought, *I know I can keep a secret. I will just enjoy his attention and not tell anyone.* I didn't tell anyone until I finally confessed all to Al.

Stinking Thinking

I was reliving old lies that had never worked in the past:

I am here to please men.

This man will make me happy.

I must keep this a secret!

Once again, the tempter had won the battle for my heart and soul.

It was Christian counseling that helped me take a look at all the lies I had been living. Caring counselors helped me see clearly that I needed to change the way I was thinking. I saw that I didn't commit adultery because I had stopped loving Al. I committed adultery because of the lies I had embraced.

When I looked at the mess of my life through the eyes of Jesus, I felt like the woman at the well. Jesus could see all her sins *and* the lies she believed that made sin seem like the best path forward.

Counseling helped me break the power of the lies that had become hardwired into my mind and heart. I accepted Jesus' love and forgiveness and asked Him to help me overcome my destructive thought patterns. And like the woman at the well, I found salvation in confession, forgiveness, and purifying my mind and heart, as the Scripture says: "If we confess our sins, he is faithful and just to forgive us our sins and to cleanse us from all unrighteousness" (1 John 1:9).

Five-Way Forgiveness

I had sinned against Al. I had sinned against God. I had sinned against my church. I had also sinned against myself by living a lie. This was a complicated mess that required five-way forgiveness.

1. Forgiveness from God

Everything changed for me when I confessed my sin of adultery to God. When I confessed and released all my desires to live life my own way, the darkness that had engulfed me lifted.

As God poured out His love and grace, my heart began to heal. The shame and guilt were melting away because of God's constant grace in my life. The lies I had lived began to fade away as they were replaced by God's truth. I experienced God's grace and love by spending time reading His Word, spending time with people who were more mature in the faith than I was, and praying with my heart wide open before God.

2. Forgiveness from Al

God promises to forgive our sins if we confess them. I had no such guarantee from Al.

My affair was a terribly personal hurt for Al, and also a terribly public humiliation. He was an associate pastor in our church of 1,500 people. He endured a painful process to come to the place where he could forgive me.

"I was completely numb," he later said. "I had warned you that I would divorce you, and when you told me about your affair, that's exactly what I felt I should do. And over the course of the next few days, weeks, and months, many people advised me to do just that."

Many of the people telling Al to divorce me quoted Scripture.

"I knew God hated divorce," he said, "but I also knew Matthew 19:9 offers a biblical justification for divorce in the case of unfaithfulness." Thank God there were other people in Al's life telling him to take some time, wait on God, and refrain from making any permanent decisions in the heat of the moment.

Al did wait, and so did I. For two months I obeyed all the boundaries that Al set. I entered our house to care for the girls, but I could not talk to him, touch him, or apologize any more. My words at this point meant nothing. In time, he could see through my life and deeds that I had changed.

"Lisa did everything the right way," he said later. "She was going through her own process as a newly forgiven Christian, and I noticed hopeful developments from afar. Lisa's friends

51

were my friends, and they told me what she was doing. She was immersing herself in Scripture and prayer. Finally, after two months, I realized that I still loved her. And to my surprise, I realized I had the capacity to forgive her."

3. Forgiveness from the Family of God

The life I lived was a textbook case of hypocrisy. On Sunday mornings I looked like a devout Christian woman. That's not the way I had lived on other days of the week. This would have been bad enough if I was just a normal believer, but as a pastor's wife, my situation was worse. I had subjected Al and his entire congregation to shame. Some members left the church, convinced that Al was out of his mind to do anything with me but divorce me and wash his hands of the whole situation.

One of the hardest things I had to do was read a letter to the entire congregation one Sunday morning. I confessed my sins, subjected myself to their judgment, and begged for their forgiveness. Thank God they had heard good sermons about God's forgiveness. They extended grace to me when I needed it the most.

4. Forgiving My Abuser

Bitterness can be a killer. The man who abused me had given me plenty to be bitter about, but my bitterness would hurt me, not him.

My counselor helped me go through exercises where I pictured my abuser sitting in an empty chair in her office.

As she guided me, I told this man how his abuse had affected me as a child, a teen, and an adult.

The counselor also helped me see that there was someone else in the office. I could begin to see Jesus there with me the whole time, extending His open arms to me. I could picture Him healing me and mending the brokenness that my abuser's sin had inflicted on me. I saw that I no longer had to see myself as a lifelong victim of that abuse. I began to see myself as a victor.

As I embraced God's love for me, I also embraced His love for this man who hurt me. That's how I was able to forgive him. We have to put ourselves in the other people's shoes, so to speak, to see life from their perspective and what may have caused them to hurt us.

But I learned that forgiveness is not the same thing as reconciliation. Al and I have decided that we do not want a relationship with this person, even though we have forgiven him. When we run into him, we can be polite, but we choose not to spend time with him. Forgiveness doesn't mean you can't have boundaries.

5. Forgiving Myself

By far the most challenging struggle in my journey of forgiveness was forgiving myself for all the needless pain and suffering I had caused everyone in my life.

In the past, I had no defense whenever Satan came and whispered his lies to me:

You are the worst sinner ever.

God can't really love you after all you have done.

There's nothing you can do to get your life back on track.

Now I overcome these attacks by running into the arms of Jesus and combating Satan's lies with God's truth. I ask Jesus to be with me and guard me. When Satan attacks me and whispers those lies, I ask God to replace them with His promises. I ask God to rebuke Satan and get him away from me. I read Scripture that tells me that I am His and He is mine. I pray for strength and light to shine on these lies. I talk with Al and with friends, who all remind me that I am forgiven by both God and Al. The more I learn to embrace God's loving forgiveness, the less attention I give to the enemy's lies.

Forgiveness and Healing Take Time

Paul makes a bold promise to us in Romans: "For I am sure that neither death nor life, nor angels nor rulers, nor things present nor things to come, nor powers, nor height nor depth, nor anything else in all creation, will be able to separate us from the love of God in Christ Jesus our Lord" (Romans 8:38-39). If none of these big powers can separate us from God's love, not even my sin could separate me from the love of God!

Experiencing forgiveness is a process, and it doesn't happen overnight. The problems I faced were decades in the making. Untangling the mess I had made of my life and marriage wouldn't happen quickly. Healing my brokenness was more complicated than microwaving a meal. This was more complicated than a TV show, where problems are fixed in half an hour.

I know some people find the whole process of confession and forgiveness too time-consuming and complicated. They would rather do what I did for years with the pains and problems inside my heart: Ignore them. Bury them. Pretend they aren't there. We saw how that worked. These unresolved pains and sorrows are fertile ground where the enemy can come in and create even more chaos and sin. Satan will use those as ticking time bombs, and he will detonate them at *his* most opportune time.

I have an important message for you, and it comes from two reliable sources: me, and the woman at the well. As you begin your own journey of experiencing forgiveness, hold on tight to the outstretched hand of God, who loves you and accepts you unconditionally.

Give yourself time. Enlist some trusted Christian friends to talk with about what you are dealing with. Seek Christian counseling to help you deal with the years of stored lies and false accusations. Stay connected at church, and don't give in to being isolated.

As you can see, forgiveness is more than a topic for me. It's my life. I pray that in the pages that follow you'll begin to grasp a picture of God's forgiving love for you. I pray that you will know the forgiveness and healing that I have known.

CHAPTER 4

HOW DESPERATE ARE YOU?

As soon as my (Al's) dad heard the quiet evening suddenly interrupted by barking, howling dogs, he suspected they had caught another intruder snooping around his home. (In my family and in the other Robertson families, dogs live *outside* the houses, where dogs are supposed to live—not inside, where they forget they are dogs and grow fat and lazy!)

After the *Duck Dynasty* TV show introduced our family to millions of viewers around the world, our homes and office became magnets for fans who loved us. Some wanted to buy a duck call in West Monroe and see the employees who made it. Others wanted our photos and autographs.

Then there were the few tenacious fans who had bigger

things on their minds. More than a few of these enterprising individuals walked up on Phil's front porch, banged loudly on his front door, and verbally assaulted him about his "judgmental" Christian beliefs or "primitive" views on homosexuality.

Dad had little patience for unexpected and unknown visitors, particularly when they came late at night. And he was prepared for whatever happened, knowing that he could not depend on local law enforcement to get to the house quickly enough to intervene in an emergency.

"I don't *call* 911," he would say. "I *am* 911!"

And on this evening, soon the sound of barking drew closer. A young man approached, climbed the steps to the front porch, and rang the doorbell.

"It's pretty late," said Phil, opening the door to the stranger while keeping his ArmaLite 15 rifle close at hand. "Are you lost?"

"No, I came down here to talk to you," said the man.

"How in the world did you get in here?" Phil asked.

"I climbed over that fence," said the man, who was breathing heavily after his climb and his encounter with the dogs.

"Why in the world would you do a fool thing like that?"

"Well, I just wanted to talk about what's going on in my life, and ask you some questions about Jesus," said the man. "My wife and our little baby are out in the car. We drove here all the way from Missouri to see you."

Phil would have quickly chased away the intruder if he was seeking only autographs or souvenirs, but I've never seen him turn away anyone who wanted to talk about Christ, no matter the hour or the circumstances.

Looking at the young man, Phil could see his single-minded commitment (he had driven more than five hundred miles in the last eight hours to get there). Phil could also sense his deep spiritual hunger. The man seemed desperate to know Jesus, and his spiritual transformation was more important to Phil than his own tiredness or the lateness or inconvenience of the visit. So he calmed down the dogs and told the man what he would do.

"Okay," he said. "I'll make you a deal. I want you to climb back over that fence, just like you climbed over it to get in here. Then you get in your car, drive to the gate, plug in the code to open the gate, and come on back here with your wife and baby. Then we'll talk."

The man asked if he could go out by the gate instead of climbing over the fence again.

"You were able to climb over pretty well the first time," said Phil. "I think you'll be able to make it just fine on your way out."

There was one final look of confusion, and then the man turned, headed for the fence, and climbed back over. Phil wasn't sure he would ever see him again after he cleared the fence, but in a minute the gate opened and the man returned, driving toward the house with his family.

Phil sat down on the front porch with the man, who said his name was Terry, while Terry's wife and child waited nearby. As Terry poured out his heart, Phil looked deep into his eyes and asked a series of probing questions about his life, his lifestyle, and his need for Christ's forgiveness. After about a half hour, everything seemed settled.

"So, you say you want to repent of your sins, accept Jesus into your life, and become a Christian right now?" Phil asked.

"I sure do," said Terry. "That's why I came down here."

"Then let me ask you a series of questions," said Phil.

"Sure."

"Son, do you believe that Jesus came to this earth to die for your sins on a cross?"

"Yes, I do, Mr. Phil."

"Do you believe that Jesus was both God and man and rose from the dead after three days?"

"Yes, I do."

"And are you willing to repent of your old, sinful ways, confess your love for Christ, and commit to following Jesus for the rest of your days here on planet Earth?"

"Yes, I do!"

"Then today is the day that your destiny changes forever, because that faith now saves you for all eternity. Welcome to the Kingdom of God, Son."

Terry sat still for a minute, taking in everything that had happened. Then he and his wife asked Phil to baptize him before they left.

Phil could never refuse a request like that. He led the couple down to the river, just as he had done countless times before, and buried Terry in a watery grave to watch him rise anew. Miss Kay was there, handing Phil and Terry dry towels and giving hugs all around.

"Don't forget," said Phil. "When you get back to Missouri, you need to get connected to a good church."

"I will," Terry said. "I will. Thank you so much for talking with me."

Terry vigorously shook Phil's hand, quickly walked back to his car, and drove away. We never saw him or heard from him again.

This encounter was just one of countless opportunities Phil and other Robertsons have had to lead spiritually hungry seekers to Christ. What made this episode memorable was Terry's willingness to climb Phil's big fence twice. That demonstrated his full-fledged commitment. This man was desperate to know Jesus, and his unusual strategy for gaining access to Phil was an impressive testimony of his devotion.

Terry was so desperate for Christ's forgiveness that he hatched a plan and pursued it with everything he had. Have you ever seen this kind of desperation for salvation and forgiveness? Have you ever experienced this kind of spiritual desperation yourself?

Such desperation isn't unusual. In fact, a group of desperate men star in one of the strangest Bible stories I've ever read.

Hole-in-the-Roof Desperation

A simple thing like a fence could never keep someone as desperate as Terry from climbing over and getting to Dad.

Likewise, people who lived at the time of Christ developed their own desperate measures to reach their Savior. For one paralyzed man, these measures included enlisting the help of four men who would carry him to the home where Jesus was speaking.

The man probably assumed his personal entourage would escort him right into Christ's presence, but that's not the way things worked out. According to this report in the Gospel of Mark, a boisterous hometown crowd complicated things even more:

> When [Jesus] returned to Capernaum after some
> days, it was reported that he was at home. And many
> were gathered together, so that there was no more
> room, not even at the door. And he was preaching
> the word to them. And they came, bringing to him
> a paralytic carried by four men.
>
> MARK 2:1-3

Can you imagine the man's frustration? Word of Jesus' compassion for the sick and His power to heal them had drawn ever-larger crowds. The paralyzed man had heard about this wandering holy man and healer. He longed to be in the front row when Jesus started performing His healing miracles.

He came up with a plan. When he proposed his unusual idea to the four local men, they agreed to help him get to the house in Capernaum. The four put him on a mat so they could carry him and set off for the house where Jesus was preaching. I can picture the four men, one on each corner of the man's mat. It must have been quite a scene as they carried the man down the city's narrow streets.

They made good progress, but once they came near the house they were shocked by what they encountered. The street looked like a mob scene from *Jesus Christ Superstar*. The crowd had spilled out of the house, and people were now surrounding the building like a human barricade, blocking the path of the four men and their patient.

Every once in a while, they could hear a word or two of Jesus' comments, but they were too far away to request divine healing. It seemed that everyone else in the city had decided to turn out for this unique event, and that everyone else had an earlier start.

Pushing and prodding, the men worked to create a path through the crowd. They were determined, but the people listening to Jesus seemed to be totally caught up in His words. There was no way the men could get through with the crowd packed as tight as sardines into the small house.

The Bible doesn't tell us much about the paralyzed man, but I can just imagine how he might have felt. If it had been me on that mat, I might have been tempted to yell out something like this: "Hey, all of you good-looking, healthy people, would you mind giving the paralyzed guy a slight break and letting us pass on through?"

I don't know if the four men tried other ways to get in. Did they circle the house seeking a window or door? Whatever they tried didn't work. And now, with the paralyzed man's frustration mounting, someone proposed that the only way in was up!

> And when they could not get near him because of the crowd, they removed the roof above him, and when they had made an opening, they let down the bed on which the paralytic lay.

MARK 2:4

I can picture the reaction: shocked looks, a few laughs, general disbelief, and snide comments. "You're crazy," I can hear them saying.

But hope and need are often stronger than doubt. Lacking any better alternatives, the men got to work, carrying the man up the steep exterior stairs that were a common feature in houses of the day. Once up on the roof, they set the man down and got to work destroying it.

Back then, people's roofs were typically constructed with big wooden support beams, smaller crossbeams and branches, layers of brush and reeds, and a mixture of mud and grass. Luke's account of this episode also mentions tiles, which were probably sun-dried mud. (See Luke 5:19.) This means that people in the room below could have been dusted with dirt, hit with chunks of mud debris, pelted with branches and beams, and even endangered by heavy falling tiles.

I would have loved to see the look on Jesus' face when

He saw what was going on. I am sure He was infinitely more patient than I am when people interrupt my teaching.

We don't know how long it took for the men to create a hole large enough to deposit their friend, but the deconstruction process must have created quite a commotion until, finally, they lowered the man down into the room and right into the presence of Jesus. Talk about special delivery!

> And when Jesus saw their faith, he said to
> the paralytic, "Son, your sins are forgiven."
> MARK 2:5

The paralyzed man's deep and desperate faith (and the faith of his friends) touched the heart of Jesus. The man had come for physical healing, but the Great Physician knew that each and every one of us also needs to experience spiritual and emotional healing.

Christ's words of forgiveness caused a stir among the teachers of the law who were opposed to Jesus and His ministry.

> Now some of the scribes were sitting there, questioning
> in their hearts, "Why does this man speak like that?
> He is blaspheming! Who can forgive sins but God
> alone?" And immediately Jesus, perceiving in his spirit
> that they thus questioned within themselves, said to
> them, "Why do you question these things in your
> hearts? Which is easier, to say to the paralytic, 'Your

sins are forgiven,' or to say, 'Rise, take up your bed and walk'? But that you may know that the Son of Man has authority on earth to forgive sins"—he said to the paralytic—"I say to you, rise, pick up your bed, and go home." And he rose and immediately picked up his bed and went out before them all, so that they were all amazed and glorified God, saying, "We never saw anything like this!"

MARK 2:6-12

Jesus responded to the teachers' unspoken charges of blasphemy by performing a miracle that confirmed His divinity. While people praised God for this miracle, I also wonder how many of the houseguests tried to get the healed man to reimburse them for dry-cleaning expenses and whether the home owners asked him to fix the roof!

Gazing into the Mirror of God's Word

Scripture is like a mirror. In the words of God's revelation, we can see our own spiritual state. The passage describing the adventures of the hole-in-the-roof gang gives us many opportunities to consider our own lives. Where do you see yourself in this story?

Perhaps there are times when you have felt like the helpless paralytic. You have a problem and believe there's a solution, but you don't experience any movement. You feel stuck. Your problem could be that you have a lifetime's worth of sin and selfishness to atone for, but you don't feel you can confront this mountain of shame. Unlike the paralytic, whose body held him back, the problem holding you back might be the hardness of your own heart. Either you don't believe you need forgiveness, or if you know you need it, you don't believe God can forgive you.

Or could you be one of the four friends who helped the paralyzed man? So many people in the world are weighed down by shame, guilt, and despair. These four rolled up their sleeves and helped the troubled man. How about you? Are you willing to help someone make that difficult journey from guilt to forgiveness? Do people who know you see you as an agent of grace, a willing soul who could help them in their time of trial, someone who loves them and cares for them and will help them find relief?

Suppose your next-door neighbor has gone through a searing spiritual crisis and is now paralyzed by guilt and fear. Are you ready and willing to be present in the mess of their life and help them find their Savior? Are you willing to witness for your faith? Are you willing to do something as simple as invite friends and neighbors to church or Bible studies, where they may experience a new lease on life? Do you make yourself available so you can serve others and help Jesus' healing words to reach many more needy seekers? Many people are desperate for Jesus, whether they know it or not. Will you help these desperate souls find hope?

Or perhaps you're one of the anonymous faces in the crowd. These people came to hear Jesus teach, but they could also see the almost comical attempts the four friends made to place the paralytic in the midst of Jesus' presence. What if you were one of the onlookers? Would you laugh at the spectacle, or would you pray that the paralyzed man finds salvation?

Perhaps you were among that crowd inside the house. People were packed together, hanging on every word from Jesus' mouth. If you had been among them, would you have sacrificed your precious real estate so the paralytic and his entourage would be able to come in? This is not a theoretical question for many churchgoing Christians. I've preached at many revival services where it seemed believers claimed all the good seats, leaving the unbelievers to stand or stay out in the cold.

Or perhaps you are more like the teachers of the law who scoffed at Jesus' power to forgive sins and looked down their noses at the common people hanging on Jesus' words. You may be well schooled in Scripture and theology, but your knowledge won't save you if you remain skeptical or even dismissive of Christ's power to heal broken people.

When Wishes Come True

I have never teamed up with three other men to lower a paralyzed man through a hole in a roof, but I came close! I was part of a four-man team that worked together to lower a disabled man into our church's baptismal pool. This was another case of desperate forgiveness. Let me tell you about Wesley, a friend who briefly came to know the Robertson clan.

Gurney Productions, the production company that produced *Duck Dynasty*, developed a relationship with the Make-A-Wish Foundation. The people at Gurney asked our family if we would like to get involved with Make-A-Wish by meeting young people who were dealing with critical illnesses and had made a final wish to meet us.

We discussed the invitation together and quickly agreed to participate. "If there's a kid who is near death, and his special wish is to see us, we say, come on, let's do it."

We arranged to host quarterly meetings with Make-A-Wish children and their families. These quarterly meetings were always somewhat chaotic, but they were also meaningful for us. It was sad to see some of the tremendous challenges these children were facing, but it was a joy to see them smiling and laughing as we fulfilled their wishes by talking to them, signing autographs, and posing for photos with them and their family members. These were days of hugs, smiles, and tears.

I was at one of these Make-A-Wish gatherings when I was introduced to Wesley. God was heavy on this young man's mind, and his heart was set on meeting Phil.

"Is Phil here?" asked a young woman who approached me and explained she was Wesley's girlfriend. She pointed to a thin, frail, pale-skinned man sitting in a wheelchair. "He wants to talk to your dad about spiritual things."

"I'm sorry," I said, "but Phil couldn't be here today. He would have loved to talk to Wesley. But would he be willing to talk with me?"

She accepted my offer of this plan B, so we arranged to meet the next morning at the church.

Wesley poured out a lifetime's list of sins, faults, failures, and bitterness. We didn't know his whole story, but what we learned was sobering. Unlike many of the other Make-A-Wish recipients, Wesley's disabilities were not the result of muscular dystrophy, cerebral palsy, or some other neuromuscular disability. He said his physical limitations were the consequences of a lifetime of wild partying and bad choices: drinking, doing drugs, and abusing his health and his body.

"I've made a lot of mistakes," Wesley told me as he laid out his litany of sorrow and bitterness.

He was as destructive to his own heart as he had been to his body. He had totally alienated all his family members and lacked any close friends. In fact, the woman who drove Wesley from Pennsylvania to meet us was actually an ex-girlfriend who had long ago lost any romantic feelings for him but was now raising their young son on her own. All she wanted was for Wesley to have the best possible life he could experience in the remaining days he had, which were expected to be few.

Wesley's heart may have been closed to other people, but it was wide open to Jesus. He accepted Christ as his Savior and then insisted he be baptized immediately. Our church has a baptistery, but we had never tried to submerge anyone in a wheelchair before.

"Wesley," I told him, "I'm going to need a little help, but I will see how we can make this happen." I explored the church high and low and came up with three additional volunteers. We wheeled him down to the front of the sanctuary, where a small group of church workers had gathered to witness the baptism. Then each one of us grabbed a limb or partial limb and gently lifted Wesley out of his chair. For a moment I felt like one of the men in Mark's Gospel.

We carried Wesley up the steps to the baptistery, and then down the steps and into the cool water. I asked him to repeat these words after me:

Lord, I've made a lot of mistakes.
I have hurt others.
I have hurt myself.
And I have closed my heart to Your love.
But now, I open my heart to You.
Please come live inside me as my Savior and
*   my Lord.*
Lord, today I confess to You that I want You to be
*   the Lord of my life, and I commit whatever time*
*   I have left to Your service.*

I held Wesley's nose closed as we lowered his limp body deeper into the water. Then we lifted him out, helped him dry off, and carried him up and out of the baptistery and back down the steps to his wheelchair, where the church workers had gathered, applauding and cheering.

As Wesley prepared to leave us, I gave him a final challenge.

"Wesley, God has given you a little bit more time. Use this time to let Him change you from the inside out. You can have a powerful impact on people, so go full bore!"

"I will, Pastor Alan," he promised me.

A few days later we heard from one of Wesley's aunts. Apparently, the love of Christ may have warmed his heart, but it failed to have any impact whatsoever on how he treated the people around him. She told us that Wesley had been given two weeks to live but would not forgive his mother, father, or brother for ways they had hurt him. He had even slammed the door in their faces.

We tried to encourage the aunt, but there was not much we could say. Then, a few weeks later, I was thrilled when she sent us a praise report saying, "God moved in Wes's heart." Wes had forgiven his family! His change of heart was bittersweet, though, because Wesley's liver was shutting down and he had only about two days to live.

His aunt expressed her thanks to me for introducing Wesley to Jesus and baptizing him, and also for our church's compassion for the lost. And she added that Wes was wearing his *Duck Dynasty* shirt that evening. I thought it was pretty funny when she wondered what type of clothing we'll all be wearing on our heavenly bodies, and then wrote, "I sure hope the Robertsons will be robed in camouflage."

Keep Being Desperate

We think the three stories in this chapter paint a vivid picture of what we mean when we talk about desperate forgiveness.

Terry was so desperate to talk to Phil about Christ that he drove for eight hours, climbed a big fence, and took a late-night dip in a cold river. You don't need to drive all the way to West Monroe, Louisiana, to confess your sins to God. But if you do make that long drive, somebody here will be more than glad to talk to you about Jesus, pray for your salvation, and baptize you, too.

Wesley's concerns about his imminent death fueled his desperation to finally clean up his life. Wesley wouldn't stop until he was forgiven. And even though his time on this earth was short, he allowed the process of forgiveness to change him from within and transform the ways he treated everyone around him.

It was a blessing to see how Wesley's newfound forgiveness spread throughout his family in the few weeks he had left to live. But you don't need to wait until your own death is near to clean up your life. Think about how much better life would have been for this family if all had been forgiven years ago.

The paralytic was so desperate for forgiveness that he hatched an elaborate plan to place himself right at the feet of Christ. But what happened next?

Over the years, we have seen many forgiven sinners rejoice, at least initially. But then time intervenes, memories grow short, and people forget what a blessing forgiveness was. They forget how God's grace transformed their lives, lifted their burdens of guilt, and empowered them to transform their broken relationships.

Our message to Christians is a simple plea: please don't quit being desperate for God's grace. Even if you have been saved for decades and are an elder or teacher in the church, you still sin and need Christ's forgiveness.

Christians also need to make sure they are not blocking other people from experiencing God's forgiveness. We wonder about all the people crammed in the house where Jesus was teaching. Yes, it's great to be there where the action is. But couldn't these people see that the paralyzed man was desperate, and they were standing between him and his Savior?

Similar things happen in churches where believers fall in love with their accustomed pew or seat in the sanctuary. We've seen believers protect their privilege rather than give up their seat for a sinner who's desperate for forgiveness.

Long story short: If you don't feel an all-consuming need for God's grace, it may be time to conduct a heart check. We're not talking about going to the doctor to be hooked up to a heart monitor. We're talking about taking a look deep inside to see what's going on in your own soul. It's possible you are overlooking sins that are keeping you from fully loving God and your neighbor.

And if people you know are desperate for forgiveness, don't block them or stand in their way. Rather, do anything you can to usher these needy souls into the healing haven of God's redemptive grace.

CHAPTER 5

"BIG" SINS,
BIG FORGIVENESS

THE SIXTEEN-YEAR-OLD GIRL WALKED into the nondescript office building on a cloudy Wednesday morning. She opened the door to one of the offices and entered a dimly lit waiting room. She gave her name to the somber-faced receptionist, who handed her a piece of paper with the number four on it.

The girl sat down in one of the chairs and stared at her hands, clutched tightly in her lap. She didn't glance up even once at the other people in the waiting room. She wasn't there to meet people or have a conversation. She was there for a single purpose, and she wanted to get it over with.

She shivered a bit in the frigid waiting room, losing track

of time until a door opened and a woman in a nurse's uniform appeared.

"Number four!" she barked.

The girl followed the nurse down a long hallway and into a small examination room.

"Okay," said the woman as she abruptly gave her orders. "You need to take everything off from the waist down, lie down on this table, and cover yourself with this sheet." The nurse exited the room as the girl undressed and lay down on the table, which was even colder than the waiting room.

When the nurse reentered the room, she immediately tried to ease the girl's anxiety. "Remember," she said, "this is just tissue. We will just remove this tissue from your body. It won't hurt, but you will probably have some cramping. After that, you won't have to think about this ever again."

Half an hour later, the girl got dressed, left the office, and went home to rest. The next morning, she went to school.

Everything is back to normal, she thought. *I don't ever need to think about this again. It was just tissue. Move on.*

A Life in Limbo

As you may have guessed, that sixteen-year-old girl was me (Lisa). The office I visited was a little hole-in-the-wall place in West Monroe. I went there seeking the best solution for the latest in my long series of problems: an unplanned pregnancy.

At the time I never even thought about whether what I was doing was right or wrong. At that point in my life, being right or wrong didn't matter. I just wanted to get the abortion done, forget about it, and get back to my normal life.

But things weren't that simple. One thing I know for sure: that nurse in the clinic lied to me when she said I wouldn't have to think about my abortion ever again. I think about it every day of my life.

The father was the boyfriend I hooked up with after Al deserted me for another girl. Al was the man of my dreams. He promised to be faithful to me. But this was a promise he couldn't keep. This was long before Al was a preacher of the gospel, and back then Al was following Satan's lead. As he would tell me later, these were the years when he was in "the devil's camp," and he pulled me down with him.

Most of the time our relationship was toxic, but being with Al was still better than all the other relationships I had been in. I believed sex was the way to keep Al in my life, but I was wrong about that. I was devastated when he moved to New Orleans. My self-esteem was shattered.

With Al gone, my life spiraled downhill for the next two years. I dabbled with drugs, drank more than my share of alcohol, and slept with various guys. My value was all wrapped up in sex, which I often confused with love.

The boyfriend who fathered my unborn child wasn't much of a father figure, or even a very nice boyfriend. He abused alcohol, drugs, and me. I knew which buttons to push, and when I did, he would hold me down and hit me. I had bruises all over my body. I could hide most of the bruises under my clothing, but it was harder to hide the anger and confusion I felt.

I endured the abuse just so I could have a relationship with someone. At the time I wasn't thinking clearly, but it seemed to me I needed the punishment. My self-image was so damaged that I subconsciously felt I needed him to hurt me. It was almost like I thought I deserved it. I didn't even think about whether it was right or wrong. It just was.

My unwanted pregnancy was an unintended consequence of the bad choices I'd been making in my life. When I decided to get an abortion, I thought this decision would take care of some of my bad choices for a while. I had stumbled into a problem, and now abortion was my way out. I wasn't happy about that, but I wasn't too upset about it either. It simply had to be done. I would never mention it again. Life would go on as if nothing had ever happened.

But there was one question I couldn't get out of my mind. It was the question I asked myself as I lay there in that ice-cold exam room, my body shivering on that sterile table.

"How Did I Get Here?"

It was desperation that brought me to the place where sex substituted for love, where killing my baby seemed like my best option to solve a problem.

My confusion about sex and love started in my childhood when a family member sexually abused me for years. I don't blame the abuse for all the mistakes I've made in life, but this experience wounded me, twisted my thinking, and warped my heart. I didn't realize it at the time, but the suffering I endured played a major role in making me believe I deserved men's abuse.

Believe it or not, during these years ours was a church-going family. If you're wondering why I didn't seek help there, that wasn't our style. As my mom always said, "You can't take that mess to church." When we went to church, we kept our sins well hidden. And since my life was one big mess, that meant I needed to stay away from all the people at church, even though they seemed to care for us.

I was young and out of control, living a wild and independent life. I would stay out all night. On occasion, my mom came blazing into town, looking for me. When she found me, she threatened to ground me, but she never followed through. All I had to do was sweet-talk my daddy, who pretty much let me do whatever I wanted. Mom would try to be a harsh disciplinarian, but I would plead my case to Daddy, and he usually let me have my way.

Daddy loved me no matter what I did, and that made him the one big exception in my life. I was his girl and I loved that. I felt special with him. The two of us had some great adventures. We would go hunting and fishing together. And during one horrible winter storm, he stayed home with me while my mom went to work. In the midst of the storm, the thrashing winds drove a piece of ice through the roof of our house, making the whole home feel intolerably cold. Daddy and I went out and sought shelter in his truck for the whole day, whiling away the hours reading, doodling, and looking at magazines. Those precious memories are dear to me, even now.

Life with Daddy was safe and free of judgment. I wish that our relationship had provided me with so much love that I didn't need to go looking for more of it in all the wrong places, but with a warped sense of worth, I was so desperate for love that I became promiscuous.

Of course, I had never even thought about getting pregnant. I only thought of the present: I wanted a man in my life, and sex kept them with me, at least for a while.

The man who fathered the child I would never know was a twenty-year-old. The fact that he was four years older than I was actually boosted my self-esteem. When I told him that a pregnancy test turned out to be positive, he was blasé.

"Well, I suppose we can just get married," he said.

"Married!" I screamed. I was desperate, but not that desperate. There was no way I wanted to marry this guy. My blinders had been taken off, and I could see clearly now. I didn't want to be with another man who abused me.

A Fetus or a Baby?

I never told my mother I was pregnant, but she noticed me getting sick every morning. She suggested that I get a pregnancy test. I must have taken three or four of them. I kept getting the same unwanted results. When I told her about the positive pregnancy test, she was upset with me. My daddy was heartbroken. His sweet little girl was suffering the consequences of having casual sex. He'd believed all the lies I'd told him. I had hurt him, and I knew he felt hurt for me too.

The way my parents saw things, a fetus doesn't become an actual baby until much later in the pregnancy process. They suggested an abortion but gave me no clues about how to get one, so I looked in the Yellow Pages section of the phone book under "abortion clinic," and there it was. Scheduling my abortion was easier than making a hair or nail appointment.

My boyfriend's family didn't want me to have an abortion, but they never offered to care for their son's child.

"It's your decision," they told me.

My boyfriend's mother did go with me to the clinic. (My mother told me she couldn't possibly take the day off work.) Their family even pitched in some money to help pay for the procedure. I added the savings I had. Just enough. Everything would be fine.

From that day on, I could never look at my boyfriend again. I was too confused to process my emotions, so I didn't understand what I was feeling. I only knew I felt terribly hurt somehow. I didn't realize it at the time, but my conscience was trying to tell me something. I had taken a life. I had sinned against my Creator. I had thrown away God's beautiful baby inside of me in some kind of failed attempt to conceal my promiscuity from the world.

I'm not the only woman to feel this way. Millions of women have had abortions in the decades after *Roe v. Wade* made the procedure legal. You may be one of those women. You may know some of these women, whose "unintended consequences" force them to make a life-or-death choice.

In my case, the relief abortion promised lasted only a moment. The regret, grief, and guilt haunted me for years. My desperation eventually led me to seek God's forgiveness. As I made this journey, I found inspiration in an unusual source.

One Night in Jerusalem

David was a devout man who wrote beautiful poems (we call them psalms) describing his love for God. By birth he was an ancestor of Jesus Christ. As King David, he ruled over Israel and Judah.

His powerful position came with many perks. One hot afternoon in Jerusalem, David abused the power of his office for his own personal gain and gratification:

> It happened, late one afternoon, when David arose
> from his couch and was walking on the roof of the
> king's house, that he saw from the roof a woman
> bathing; and the woman was very beautiful. And
> David sent and inquired about the woman. And one
> said, "Is not this Bathsheba, the daughter of Eliam, the
> wife of Uriah the Hittite?" So David sent messengers
> and took her, and she came to him, and he lay with
> her. (Now she had been purifying herself from her
> uncleanness.) Then she returned to her house.
>
> 2 SAMUEL 11:2-4

Sometimes being the king can get lonely. David had already lay down for a rest, but perhaps the warm breezes of springtime roused him and brought him outside to the roof. From this elevated perch he saw her: a beautiful, naked babe, bathing alone on her terrace. Her beauty stunned him, so he asked one of his many subordinates who she was.

She was the wife of one of David's loyal soldiers, Uriah the Hittite. David's armies were far off, fighting the Ammonites and other enemies. Now Uriah's enticing wife was on her own at home. I can picture the battle going on inside David's heart.

Wow, she is gorgeous!

But on the other hand, she's Uriah's wife. Forbidden fruit.

But I am king! I can do what I want. No one can stop me.

I better go back inside and stop tempting myself.

Wow, she is gorgeous!

He summoned royal messengers to carry out his dirty work. The messengers may have wondered about the ethics of their assignment, but an order is an order. No one contradicted the king.

Bathsheba was shocked to see her restful evening interrupted by an imperial summons, but she couldn't contradict the king either, so she departed for the palace with the messengers as ordered. She might have thought that David had word concerning Uriah—maybe he was dead or sick.

David's Unintended Consequence

A short time later Bathsheba made an important discovery: "And the woman conceived, and she sent and told David, 'I am pregnant'" (2 Samuel 11:5).

What would the neighbors think? Everyone knew Bathsheba's husband was an honorable soldier who had been gone for months, fighting for the king in distant lands. Uriah the Hittite could not have fathered this child.

I can imagine Bathsheba's conflicting thoughts.

I never should have let him touch me.

But how could I have stopped him? I'll never know.

I've longed for a child, longed to be a mother, but now I will live in shame.

David's servants knew what had happened, but word had not yet spread through the kingdom. David may have thought:

Oh, what a fool I was. Now I must take care of this. I need to cover this up.

I need to call Uriah home so he can sleep with Bathsheba. Then my baby will seem to be his baby.

That should take care of things.

David put his devious cover-up into motion, having Uriah brought to him under the pretense of requesting a firsthand account of the war. After the meeting, David dismissed Uriah, assuming he would go home for the night and sleep with Bathsheba. But Uriah was an honorable servant of the king and leader of his men. He refused to go home and be with his wife while his soldiers were still dying in battle.

Now David was caught in a jam.

Oh, my. Uriah is so honorable that he won't go home for the night.

Time for plan B.

The Plot Thickens

David put his cover-up 2.0 into action the very next day.

> In the morning David wrote a letter to Joab and sent
> it by the hand of Uriah. In the letter he wrote, "Set
> Uriah in the forefront of the hardest fighting, and
> then draw back from him, that he may be struck
> down, and die." And as Joab was besieging the city,
> he assigned Uriah to the place where he knew there
> were valiant men. And the men of the city came
> out and fought with Joab, and some of the servants
> of David among the people fell. Uriah the Hittite
> also died.
>
> 2 SAMUEL 11:14-17

Can you picture David plotting an innocent man's death as part of his effort to cover up his own sexual sin? That's how evil festers and grows. What started with lust mutated into murder.

I can imagine it: I snuffed out an innocent baby's life to cover up my own sexual sin!

One of David's most famous psalms sounds like it could be his confession to God after these events:

For my iniquities have gone over my head;
    like a heavy burden, they are too heavy for me.
My wounds stink and fester
    because of my foolishness,
I am utterly bowed down and prostrate;
    all the day I go about mourning.
For my sides are filled with burning,
    and there is no soundness in my flesh.
I am feeble and crushed;
    I groan because of the tumult of my heart.

PSALM 38:4-8

David's Desperate Forgiveness, and Mine

I can understand David's pain and sorrow. My own promiscuity led me to a desperate place. I was not an all-powerful king like David but merely a lost, love-hungry teenager. Even so, my sin was equal to David's. I dispensed with a human life to cover up a "problem" of my own making.

Yet the abortion created new problems. From the time I was sixteen until the time I was thirty-five, I felt a painful sorrow for what I had done. My guilt overwhelmed me. Without healing, my emotional wounds festered.

I struggled to forgive myself, crying out to God as David did in another of his desperate psalms:

Have mercy on me, O God,
    according to your steadfast love;
according to your abundant mercy

> blot out my transgressions.
> Wash me thoroughly from my iniquity,
>   and cleanse me from my sin!
> For I know my transgressions,
>   and my sin is ever before me.

PSALM 51:1-3

My sins followed me into my marriage to Al, and my guilt colored my emotions each time Al and I tried to have a child. Our first baby came at twenty-nine weeks, weighing only one pound, fifteen ounces. Our second baby almost came at twenty-six weeks, but a medical procedure allowed me to carry her to full term. Our third pregnancy lasted only three months, ending in a miscarriage. I thought I knew *exactly* why I was having these problems. *God is angry at me for taking the life of my baby, and now He is punishing me. He's using these pregnancies to pay me back.*

It wasn't until I fell to the ground in our backyard under the weight of all this sin and confessed my unfaithfulness to Al that I finally experienced and accepted God's love and forgiveness for me. Looking back now, I can see how my failure to receive God's forgiveness all those years robbed me of experiencing the love that both Jesus and Al tried to offer me. My guilt kept me from feeling worthy of *anyone's* love. I had heard thousands of times that Christ had taken everyone's sins to the Cross to secure our forgiveness. But this was just theology and theory before desperation forced me to go to the Cross myself.

Maybe it's the same for you. You've heard Christ died for your sins. But do you believe it? Do you trust it? Are you willing to confess your sins to Him and receive His forgiveness? Don't close your heart to God's forgiveness. He loves you enough to forgive every single sin you have committed.

Cry out to Him in desperation like David did. Like I did.

I spent nearly twenty years hiding from God's love and mercy, thinking my sins were too big and too bad for God to forgive. I carried my burdens deep inside, refusing to share them with anyone and distancing myself from my Creator and the man I loved. I was desperate, but not forgiven. I thank God that my defenses finally gave way, allowing me to experience the cleansing power of His love.

Three Women, Three Choices

What would you do if you faced the challenge of an unwanted pregnancy? What would you do if your daughter came to you with a big secret?

Most people think, *This can never happen to me.* But it happens to millions of girls and women.

Women have three basic choices when faced with this dilemma. I know three women who chose three different options. All three were sixteen years old when they faced their terrible decisions. All three were unwed and pregnant and did not have a personal relationship with Christ.

Girl #1 was Miss Kay. She and Phil were teenagers in love when they had sex and she became pregnant. Although she did not have a deep Christian faith at the time, Miss Kay chose life. She gave birth to a beautiful baby boy named Al, who became my life. She loved Al and cared for him as she completed high school and waited for Phil to complete college and start a career so they could be married and raise a family. You can imagine how grateful I am that my mother-in-law chose life for her baby boy.

Girl #2 was Kate. She loved her boyfriend deeply and gave herself to him. A short time later she was pregnant. Unfortunately, her life circumstances made it difficult for Kate to raise that baby herself. As a high-school junior, she was too unprepared for motherhood. Her own mother was chronically ill, meaning Kate would have limited support from her family. All these factors led her to a crucial decision. She chose life, but chose to let a childless couple adopt and raise her baby. Kate still feels some regret about her decision but feels she did the best she could at the time.

Girl #3 was in emotional turmoil, having lost the love of her life, which had left her brokenhearted. She fell into a lifestyle filled with poor choices. Even though she still carried a torch for her absent ex-boyfriend, she had sex with other boyfriends and became pregnant. She attended church but couldn't bring herself to share her problems with anyone there. Her shame was too great.

Girl #3 was me. I chose death for my child: death for the life living inside of me, death to the future generations that could have been born, death to one of God's precious children. I thought my decision would end my "problem," but I still live with the painful consequences of that decision every day.

Like David in Psalm 51, I cried out for God to have mercy on me according to His steadfast love, to blot out my sin that I felt was ever before me.

I made a choice that was life-altering for myself and life-ending for my baby. I make no excuses for my choice. Yes, there were factors beyond my control that influenced my choice, but it was still my choice to make. And that's true for any woman today facing a similar decision.

I believed I had to face my decision on my own without help from anyone else. I realize now I was fatally wrong about that. I hope that you never find yourself in a similar predicament, but if you do, I hope you'll reach out to someone who cares, and choose life.

From Shunning to Supporting

Half a century ago, girls who got pregnant were "bad girls" who "got in trouble," and the only way to save face for families and solve these "problems" was to send the girls off to a home or orphanage where they could deliver their babies in privacy before returning to life as "normal."

At the time, people believed shame was good, and in some cases, the more the better. Shame was the all-powerful tool that might scare these bad girls away from getting into trouble again later on. The worse they felt about themselves the better, because that shame was believed to be some kind of insurance against future moral failures.

That approach didn't work too well, and then abortion was made legal in the United States in 1973. It was a new day, with new freedoms for women to end their pregnancies. *Roe v. Wade* also signaled the start of a decades-long culture war over abortion.

Christians send mixed messages to women who wrestle with unintended pregnancies. On the one hand, we teach that each life is beautiful and loved by God. But on the other hand, we don't always embody that love when we talk to women about these important life issues. Many Christians believe that abortion is murder, and as a result, they treat women like me as murderers.

Some Christians still seem to believe that shame and judgment are the best ways to change a woman's heart. They believe that reaching out and showing love and compassion to "bad girls" like me actually encourages us to become even worse. They believe that such compassion could even cause "good" girls to become "bad" girls who have children outside of marriage. According to these "blame game" Christians, shame and guilt are necessary to keep people from acting out their sexual desires. They fear that treating "bad" girls with love and compassion would send the message that premarital and extramarital sex are permissible, or even good.

Shame is powerful, but I don't believe it keeps girls from sin. Rather, it keeps girls *trapped* in sin. Shame causes many people to be wracked by guilt over their sexual sins. For these women, sexual sin becomes the unforgivable sin—or at least they *think* it's unforgivable.

We meet many Christian women who struggle with the same kinds of guilt, stigma, and social isolation I dealt with. Al and I meet many of these desperate women when we speak to groups about our journey of desperate forgiveness. Their grief and sorrow can be almost overpowering.

Yet I understand them, and their stories resonate with me. They remind me of myself before I experienced my own case of desperate forgiveness, and like them, I was burdened by the weight of my sorrow and guilt. It's amazing to tell these tortured souls the good news I have experienced: Christ can forgive your sins, even the sin of abortion.

Agents of God's Grace

I have experienced desperation, and I have known desperate forgiveness. I am grateful for the grace God showered on me after I confessed my abortion. I now want to be an agent of God's grace to others. I want to be a grace-giver who tells hurting women that God can set them free, just as He did with me.

If you have not experienced this grace yourself, your heavenly Father is waiting to heal and forgive you. But if you *have* experienced this grace, I invite you join me as a fellow grace-giver. God knows there are many women who need grace!

Because of our own experience, Al and I are passionate about working with and supporting various groups and ministries that promote life. We encourage you to get to know the following organizations, find out what they do, and see how you can help:

- Embrace Grace provides emotional, practical, and spiritual support for single young women and their families who find themselves in an unintended pregnancy. (https://embracegrace.com)

- Obria offers an app that can be downloaded, as well as pregnancy tests, STD testing, prenatal care, counseling, ultrasounds, and well-women care. We met the founder of this organization. She is a post-abortive woman, too. (https://www.obria.org)

- National Life Center (1-800-848-5683)

- America's Crisis Pregnancy Helpline (1-800-672-2296)

- Heartbeat International's website offers a worldwide directory of pregnancy centers. (https://www.heartbeat international.org)

To find a local pregnancy center, visit https://optionline .org and type in your zip code. Most pregnancy centers offer pregnancy tests, STD tests, counseling, child-raising classes, and assistance choosing an adoption center—if that's the choice a woman makes. Most will also help a woman throughout her pregnancy and as she begins raising her child.

All life is from God. All life is important to God. We hope that you will choose life and encourage others to do the same.

But remember, all is not lost for women who fall into the

same kinds of sexual sin that I experienced. God's grace is vast, and if we repent, His forgiveness is plenty big enough to overcome and forgive even the biggest and baddest of our sins.

CHAPTER 6

FORGIVENESS FOR
THE DOUBLE-MINDED

You never know who you're going to run into at a Bible study, as we discovered one December night in 1991 when a man named Matt Owens walked into the study we hosted in our home for a few friends and family members. Matt was a local who knew some of the Robertson boys, and he had just turned twenty-one. When we asked him to describe his own personal spiritual state, he summarized it like this: "I am a good old boy who gets drunk and sleeps around, but I haven't murdered anybody!"

Later in the discussion, we asked Matt if he could tell us what he thought the gospel was all about. He seemed unsure and asked, "Are you talking about gospel music? I guess that would be singing the gospel, right?"

Then Al asked the question evangelists have long employed: "If Jesus came back tonight, where would you stand? Would you be among Christ's disciples?"

"That's a pretty valid question right there," said Matt. "I had always thought I was saved, going back to when I raised my hand in a church service. I didn't know what I was doing at the time, but I knew I didn't want to go to hell. So, was I converted? I don't really know."

The Bible study wrapped up after a couple of hours, but Matt and Al continued talking late into the night, with Al asking a series of probing questions. Sometime after midnight, Matt made his confession.

"Al, I don't know the answers to a lot of the questions you're asking me, but I will tell you this much. After listening to everything you said, I realize I'm lost."

"Well," asked Al, "do you want to be saved?"

"I'm ready to go," said Matt. "Al, if you have the keys to that church building, can you baptize me tonight for the forgiveness of all my sins?"

"Sure," said Al.

The two walked next door to the church, and the impact of the evening was immediate, as Matt experienced a new life in Christ.

"As soon as I came up out of that water, I felt free, cleansed, and clear," said Matt. "I went home that night and laid there in bed feeling as light as a feather. It was like a ton of bricks had been taken off my shoulders. There was no more guilty conscience."

The Power of Pride

The people at our church embraced Matt, and he embraced us back, attending services on Sunday morning, a house church on Sunday night, and our Bible study on Wednesday nights. For the next year and a half, he was at church just about every time those church doors opened.

But by 1993, something troubling was happening with Matt.

"I had grown up as a dumb country kid, and by the age of twenty-one, I had never read a book from cover to cover," he said. "But now I started reading all I could get my hands on. I would read the Bible, commentaries, and books about the Bible. I sometimes had three books going at one time, with a dictionary to help me, and I just loved it. There was so much I wanted to learn."

Matt began spending a lot of time with Phil, and the two debated religion and philosophy while Phil made duck calls.

"I was reading, studying, and picking a lot of stuff up, and everybody was amazed at how much I knew so quickly. But I was getting prideful about it and seeking out arguments with anyone who would talk to me."

Phil had been studying the Bible for years, while Matt had only been a Christian for two years. Still, Matt offered to educate Phil on Scripture.

"Phil," Matt offered, "if you have any questions about religion or the Bible, I can answer them."

Phil didn't accept Matt's offer, but he could tell Matt was struggling. *This man is so arrogant!* Phil thought.

Even when Matt sought to evangelize others and introduce them to Christ, he often focused more on winning the debate rather than helping people experience the love and forgiveness of Christ. Over time, his faith became increasingly rule-based and legalistic, even after he decided to study at a seminary.

"When I was attending seminary, I would lie in bed worrying about my salvation," Matt said. "As I was falling asleep, I would wonder, *What if I haven't repented of sin from today, and I die in my sleep and go to hell?*" He would then quickly jump out of bed and pray for forgiveness.

"If I was driving down Interstate 55 toward Memphis, and I was going one mile over the speed limit, I would worry, *What if I get in a wreck, and God condemns me for breaking the speed limit and I go to hell?* Then I would pull over to the side of the highway and repent."

The more Matt read the Bible, the more he saw it as God's big rule book, and his goal was to rigorously obey all the rules he could while aggressively challenging everyone else he met and condemning them for not following the rules sufficiently.

"I came to believe that other Christians were completely screwed up," said Matt. "I thought that my pickup truck could have held all the people in the world I believed were going to heaven. I had everything narrowed down real tightly."

Matt started attending a different church, as well as a seminary that focused on Bible memorization, debate, and apologetics, which is the rational defense of the Christian faith. But the more he learned, they more prideful he became about all that he knew.

"I was taking college classes," said Matt, "and my goal was to get a PhD not only for the learning but also because I thought that the degree would put me in a position where people couldn't question me. It was a confusing time. Originally, I believed the blood of Jesus had saved me, but now I thought that as long as I knew enough Scripture, I didn't have to worry about anything else. If I knew enough Bible verses by heart, I wouldn't fall. But that was where the pride really came in."

Matt seemed unaware of Peter's suggestion to embrace humility instead of pride: "Humble yourselves, therefore, under the mighty hand of God so that at the proper time he may exalt you, casting all your anxieties on him, because he cares for you. Be sober-minded; be watchful. Your adversary the devil prowls around like a roaring lion, seeking someone to devour" (1 Peter 5:6-8).

The Devil and the Double-Minded

The devil made a feast out of Matt, who finally realized there was no way he could keep all the rules he read about in the Bible. He eventually rejected Christ, walked away from church, and returned to his good-old-boy ways with a vengeance. It would be nearly fourteen years before we saw Matt again.

How can it be that someone who has experienced the saving forgiveness of Christ winds up later rejecting that same forgiveness and returning to his former life of sin? It's an important question, and one the Bible addresses directly.

Peter warned about human pride and a devouring devil, and as we all know, Peter had his own issues with pride and doubt. Most famously, Peter rejected Christ three times. This famous disciple had enjoyed constant contact with Jesus, having a front-row seat for three of the most amazing years that have ever occurred on planet Earth. But still, he denied Christ when a time of challenge came.

Matt and Peter lived two thousand years apart from each other, but they shared a powerful connection. Both struggled with a potentially fatal condition that the apostle James called double-mindedness. James addressed the problem twice in his brief letter, first in James 1:6-8: "The one who doubts is like a wave of the sea that is driven and tossed by the wind. For that person must not suppose that he will receive anything from the Lord; he is a double-minded man, unstable in all his ways."

James said it's our passions and worldly desires that fuel our double-mindedness and pride: "Therefore it says, 'God opposes the proud but gives grace to the humble.' Submit yourselves therefore to God. Resist the devil, and he will flee from you. Draw near to God, and he will draw near to you.

Cleanse your hands, you sinners, and purify your hearts, you double-minded" (James 4:6-8).

What is it that makes double-mindedness so dangerous? We've seen it play out many times. These are some of the key dangers:

- *Destructive doubt.* All believers experience questions about their faith and moments of doubt. But double-minded people often drown in doubt, unable to cling to saving faith. As James put it, the double-minded person is "driven and tossed by the wind" and "unstable in all his ways."

- *Lack of trust in God.* Growing as a Christian requires believers to exercise trust in God, relying on Him for strength and guidance. But the double-minded person finds it difficult to trust God. Both Matt and Peter often trusted themselves more than they trusted God.

- *A haven for hypocrisy.* Double-minded people often say one thing but do the opposite, which is the dictionary definition of *hypocrisy*. Matt started out believing he was using his knowledge and debate skills to win people to the Lord, but over time the only thing he cared about was winning arguments. "I had the attitude of, *Hey, you can't talk to me—look at who I am and how smart I am!* I was building walls between people, not pulling the walls down!"

- *Logic vs. love.* Paul reasoned with the intellectuals of Athens (see Acts 17), and Christian teachers and preachers have used reasoning ever since. God calls many of His servants to do intellectual work. But Christianity is not primarily a system of thought or worldview. It's a way of life, and it takes more than correct theology to faithfully follow Christ.

Peter and Matt both struggled with double-mindedness for much of their lives, and both suffered the consequences. Let's see how these two men gave in to double-mindedness before learning how to transcend it with God's grace.

Peter's Problems

Peter was one of the original twelve disciples and one of the key leaders of the early church. But Peter was also double-minded, overly emotional, often impulsive, and frequently stressed out, as we can see in the many stories in the Gospels that feature him.

Many people have attempted to psychoanalyze Peter using modern psychiatric tools and categories. For example, the ministry responsible for *The Jesus Film* used the Myers-Briggs personality test lingo to portray Peter as an ENFP, which means he was an extroverted, intuitive feeler and perceiver. Peter could be zealous one moment and afraid the next, impulsive one moment and cautious the next. He was also easily overwhelmed and overcome by shame over his own personal failures.[1]

No personality type is perfect, but we can clearly see Peter's character defects in some of his key episodes with Jesus.

Portrait of Peter #1

In Matthew 14, we see Peter's double-mindedness in dramatic detail. His faith and his doubt are at war within him, throwing everything he does into disarray.

After another long day of preaching to the crowds near a lake, Jesus sent the people away and went up on a mountain where He could be by Himself and pray to His father. Meanwhile, the disciples took the boat to the other side of the lake.

Later that evening, Jesus walked on the water to reach the boat, freaking out some of the disciples.

"It is a ghost!" said one.

"Take heart," said Jesus. "It is I. Do not be afraid."

After Peter saw his master perform this marine miracle, he couldn't wait to try it himself.

"Lord," Peter said, "if it is you, command me to come to you on the water."

Peter started walking on the water toward Jesus, but he didn't get far before he became afraid of the wind and waves and began to sink.

"Lord, save me," Peter cried out.

Jesus saved Peter, but not without criticizing him for his double-mindedness.

"O you of little faith, why did you doubt?" (See Matthew 14:22-33.)

Portrait of Peter #2

After miraculously feeding five thousand people with some loaves of bread and a few fish, Jesus asked His disciples what kind of reports they were hearing from the people.

"Who do people say that the Son of Man is?" He asked.

The reports were all over the place, with some people comparing Jesus to John the Baptist, and others saying He was a modern-day Elijah or Jeremiah.

"But who do you say that I am?" Jesus asked the men who had been with Him from the beginning.

At this point, you can see Peter raising his hand to answer, just like a know-it-all student in a middle-school classroom.

"You are the Christ, the Son of the living God," Peter said.

It was a great answer, and Jesus lavished His praise on Peter for his faith.

"Blessed are you!" Jesus told Peter. "For flesh and blood has not revealed this to you, but my Father who is in heaven. And I tell you, you are Peter, and on this rock I will build my church, and the gates of hell shall not prevail against it. I will give you the keys of the kingdom of heaven, and whatever you bind on earth shall be bound in heaven, and whatever you loose on earth shall be loosed in heaven."

For a brief moment, Peter basked in the praise. But then a short time later, Peter's faith was not so strong. Jesus explained to His disciples that there would be tough times ahead. Jesus said He must go to Jerusalem, suffer much pain and indignity, and ultimately be killed before rising again from the dead.

Peter wanted nothing to do with any of this.

"Far be it from you, Lord! This shall never happen to you."

Jesus quickly took Peter aside and set him straight, accusing him of following Satan.

"Get behind me, Satan! You are a hindrance to me. For you are not setting your mind on the things of God, but on the things of man." (See Matthew 16:13-23.)

Portrait of Peter #3

Finally, all of the horrible things Jesus had told His disciples would happen began happening. He went to Jerusalem, where Judas betrayed Him. Jesus would meet death by crucifixion, and He warned that things would get tougher on His disciples.

"This very night you will all fall away on account of me," He told them.

But Peter wouldn't hear it. "Even if all fall away on account of you, I never will."

Jesus looked straight at Peter and rebuffed him. "Truly I tell you, this very night, before the rooster crows, you will disown me three times."

Again, Peter doubted his master and trusted in his own strength. "Even if I have to die with you, I will never disown you."

We all know what happened later. After Jesus took Peter and a couple of other disciples to Gethsemane to pray with Him, the disciples fell asleep. This set the stage for Peter's three denials.

First, a servant girl came to Peter. "You also were with Jesus of Galilee," she said.

"I don't know what you're talking about," Peter replied.

Soon another servant girl saw him and pointed him out to the crowd. "This fellow was with Jesus of Nazareth."

"I don't know the man!" Peter said, swearing an oath.

Then some of the crowd approached Peter, claiming he was one of the disciples. "Surely you are one of them; your accent gives you away."

"I don't know the man!" Peter swore.

Matthew's report closes with this sad conclusion: "Immediately a rooster crowed. Then Peter remembered the word Jesus had spoken: 'Before the rooster crows, you will disown me three times.' And he went outside and wept bitterly." (See Matthew 26:31-75, NIV.)

Matt's Double-Minded Life

Matt disappeared from our lives for more than a decade, but we never forgot about him during his tumultuous time. After graduating from seminary, he preached guest sermons at churches in the South, making a name for himself as a fiery debater and defender of "the truth," as he understood it. Unfortunately, he was railing against sin in his sermons but engaging in sin in a secret life that church leaders didn't know about. Like Peter, double-minded Matt was denying Christ in both word and deed. He had more important things on his mind. First on his list was sex.

"I still believed in God, and I still knew the Bible was

true," said Matt, "but I got wrapped up in sin after meeting a perfect girl at the driving range I operated. In time, I was sleeping with whoever I could get my hands on."

It's ironic, but Matt's three intense years as an intellectual-warrior Christian had enhanced his ability to seduce women.

"Before I got saved, whenever I would talk to girls, I would get tongue-tied and mumble like Elmer Fudd. Now that I had been to seminary and studied debate, I could talk *really well*, and I used my new skills with the ladies."

Occasionally, Matt would be reminded of his previous life by a moving gospel song on the radio or a preacher quoting the Bible on TV—but he would quickly turn away. People invited Matt to come back to church or Bible study, but he either didn't answer or rudely declined.

What an idiot God is for trying to bring me back! he thought.

In time came a series of arrests, beginning with the time Matt was driving drunk one New Year's Eve and ran out of gas on the highway outside of Houston. He promptly called 911 and asked for a refill. A while later, police officers showed up.

"I really appreciate you boys getting me some gas," said Matt, who quickly failed a sobriety test and then spent the night in jail.

Not surprisingly, his second arrest was also for driving under the influence. The next was for possession of cocaine. Even though Matt was guilty once again, these charges were later dropped due to a technicality, but Matt's story and photo were splashed all over the local newspaper and news programs.

Matt was supposedly living a life of pleasure and excitement, but the thrill was gone.

"I wasn't broke yet financially, but I had definitely hit rock bottom personally," he said. "The way I felt, I didn't want to see anybody. I just hated everybody."

Matt's Journey Home

Matt's turning point finally came in the fall of 2013. He was sitting at the bar in the Downtown Lounge in West Monroe, snorting cocaine and downing glasses of Crown Royal whiskey. That was when he saw his old friend Phil Robertson talking on the television.

Duck Dynasty had been a popular TV show for years, but it was generating controversy and calls for boycotts after Phil allegedly made "hateful" comments about homosexuality. Phil doesn't hate anybody, but in an interview he gave to *GQ* magazine, he said he believed homosexuality was a sin, and that his belief was based on biblical teaching.

The LGBT community reacted quickly, calling for a boycott of *Duck Dynasty*. A&E, the cable network that broadcast the show, announced that Phil had been "indefinitely" suspended. Soon, all kinds of groups rose up to defend Phil, raising the temperature of the debate even more.

The controversy got Phil a lot of press coverage, including the evening news show that Matt watched through bleary eyes that evening in the bar. Seeing Phil defending his beliefs on Fox News stirred up Matt's old argumentative instincts.

"I know the verses Phil is quoting," Matt said to the man

next to him in the bar. Then Matt, who had not opened a Bible in more than a decade, recited from memory this passage in Paul's letter to the Corinthians: "Or do you not know that the unrighteous will not inherit the kingdom of God? Do not be deceived: neither the sexually immoral, nor idolaters, nor adulterers, nor men who practice homo-sexuality, nor thieves, nor the greedy, nor drunkards, nor revilers, nor swindlers will inherit the kingdom of God" (1 Corinthians 6:9-10).

The man was surprised to hear a drunken cokehead spout Scripture, but Matt was just getting started. He followed his Scripture recitation with a meandering confession.

"Everybody gets all bent out of shape about men who have sex with men," Matt told the man, "but aside from that particular sin, I've done pretty much every other sin on that list. The devil got me and tricked me. He took some-thing that's good—studying the Bible and learning how to debate—and seduced me into becoming prideful about it. And when I couldn't live up to my own rigid rulebook, I fell for all the oldest, stupidest sins in the book.

"Look at me! I'm the sorriest dude in this whole bar. I'm lost. I'm not going to inherit the Kingdom of God."

Welcoming the Prodigal Home

Some of the Robertsons ran into Matt a few months later while taping an episode of *Duck Dynasty*.

"Hey, Matt," said Jep. "Phil wants you to come see him sometime."

Matt had been avoiding Phil like the plague, but this broke the ice, so he went.

"All right, Owens," said Phil. "Where've you been?"

The two commenced talking about God and the Bible, just like they had last done years earlier. It felt good for both of them, but Phil had something he'd been wanting to say to Matt for a long, long time.

"Owens," Phil said as he looked Matt in the eye, "you've got the facts down right—you just need to start following Jesus."

Matt's response surprised us. Instead of arguing and debating, he acknowledged Phil was right.

"That hits home with me," said Matt. "I once had some four thousand religion books in my library, but I forgot all about the relationship I needed to have with God. I want to focus on that relationship with Christ now."

The Robertson household responded to this heartfelt confession the only way we knew how: with a big welcome-home party for the returning prodigal.

"Okay," said Phil, "get those rib eyes out. Everyone in this house who has repented of sin gets a steak tonight."

"Grill that fatted calf," hollered Jase. "Owens is back."

Jesus Never Says, "Three Strikes and You're Out!"

Peter wept bitterly after denying Christ three times. The Bible doesn't tell us how long the crying went on, but we suspect the tears may have kept falling for some time as Peter reflected on his double-mindedness and frequent failures.

Americans may be familiar with laws for habitual criminal

offenders called "three strikes" laws. The name refers to base-ball, where three strikes means the batter is out. The law's purpose is to lock up violent offenders who have two previ-ous convictions. There's no grace or legal leeway for criminals after the third strike, with many of these laws calling for mandatory life sentences in prison.

Thank God that Christ doesn't enforce three-strikes laws against habitual sinners, because all of us would be in a heap of trouble. Jesus actually showed His love for Peter after His resurrection by giving Peter a chance to hit three home runs, as we see in the Gospel of John:

> When they had finished breakfast, Jesus said to Simon Peter, "Simon, son of John, do you love me more than these?" He said to him, "Yes, Lord; you know that I love you." He said to him, "Feed my lambs." He said to him a second time, "Simon, son of John, do you love me?" He said to him, "Yes, Lord; you know that I love you." He said to him, "Tend my sheep." He said to him the third time, "Simon, son of John, do you love me?" Peter was grieved because he said to him the third time, "Do you love me?" and he said to him, "Lord, you know everything; you know that I love you."
>
> JOHN 21:15-17

What was Jesus doing here? Was He trying to give Peter a chance to replace his three denials with three affirmations of his love? Was He trying to offer up easy pitches that Peter could hit out of the park? That wouldn't surprise us a bit.

God Sees the Tears of the Desperate

In Matt Owens's case, the crying continued for a long, long time after he had come back to Christ.

"Pretty much every day for the next six months, I would get down on my hands and knees and just pray and cry," Matt says. "I was crying about how wonderful it was that God would take me back after all I had done. I could see all the rotten stuff I had done, and how I'd abused all the good things God had given me. But I knew deep down I was forgiven."

Matt once dreamed about speaking to huge crowds of one hundred thousand or more, but he's now content to facilitate small Bible studies or work anonymously alongside church planters who are starting new congregations.

When Matt gave his testimony at a local church one night, he thanked God for rescuing him, referring to his sinfulness in colorful terms. Matt's language was probably more graphic than the host pastor wanted, but his honest confession did bring a few people to the altar after the sermon to confess their sins.

Back when Matt's faith was fueled by pride and book knowledge, he didn't really believe he needed Christ's forgiveness to save him. But after his long run as a prodigal, he finally came to his place of desperation. Now he's glad to help others on their journeys home.

As we worked on this chapter about the sins of the double-minded person, we heard Matt talk about the changes he had experienced on his own desperate journey.

"I actually listen to people now instead of trying to hit them over the head with a big verbal hammer," he told us. "And sometimes when people ask me questions, like, 'How could God permit such a horrible thing as X or Y?' I just tell them that sometimes I don't know. It feels so good to admit that I don't know it all. What a relief!"

Your Peter Moments

When we speak to groups about forgiveness and teach on this passage, we often ask people if they can picture Peter weeping bitterly. Then we ask them if they can relate to Peter's sorrow and remorse.

Have you ever wept bitterly over your own failures and sins?

Have you ever been double-minded, saying you love Christ with your mouth but denying Him with your actions?

What is it that has made you cry tears of remorse and sorrow?

How did you feel while you were weeping bitterly? And how did you feel afterward?

We've certainly had our seasons of bitter weeping, and while they were no fun, we thank God for these times that showed us—once again—our need for desperate forgiveness.

CHAPTER 7

PUT DOWN
YOUR STONES

WE WERE WORKING TOGETHER AT the church one Wednesday afternoon when a phone call came in. The receptionist said it was Trey Tomlinson, a close friend of ours and a faithful member of White's Ferry Road Church for thirty years.

"It sounds serious," the receptionist warned Al, who picked up the phone in our office.

"Trey, how are you doing?" Al asked.

"Al! I need to talk to you!" Trey quickly said, his voice loud enough that I (Lisa) could almost hear his words.

"Sure," said Al. "Whatever you want to—"

Trey interrupted. "Al," he said, "Anna's having an affair!"

"An affair?" Al replied. "Oh, my!"

Anna, Trey's wife, was a faithful, longtime member of our church too. Al and I knew the couple well, and we had helped them during earlier rough spots in their marriage.

Trey had suffered some painful things in his past, including the death of his mother at an early age. He had struggled with tough problems from his upbringing, pornography, and drinking. He'd been working on all of these issues, and we thought he and Anna were doing well. Apparently they weren't.

Anna had faced some issues herself. Lisa had talked with her about her poor self-esteem. Anna was always superthin, and she wore lots of makeup. Her looks were extremely important to her, and she seemed to need a great deal of affirmation. But it seemed she never received *enough* affirmation, and she continued to struggle with self-doubt and insecurities. Anna was only seventeen when she married Trey, who was thirty-two, divorced from his first wife, and already the father of two children from that marriage. After they married, Trey and Anna had two young children of their own.

Over the years we had seen Trey and Anna overcome many of their problems in life and in their marriage, but now the marriage seemed to be threatened with infidelity.

Al talked to Trey for half an hour. Afterward, we sat down and came up with a game plan.

"This Sounds Bad"

Al described his conversation with Trey to me.

"This sounds bad," said Al, shaking his head in disbelief. "It sounds like Anna has temporarily lost it."

We agreed that the two of us would meet with Anna to hear her side of the story. Even though we trusted Trey, we had learned long ago never to make any determinations about who has been doing what in a relationship without hearing from both participants. Plus, our own battles with infidelity and other challenges had taught us how complex marital problems can be, and how both husbands and wives harbor brokenness and weakness that can potentially threaten their marriages.

For me, the commitment to hear Anna's story before making any judgments sprang not only from my personal experiences but also from my study of the Bible, which shows that even good men can fall into sexual sin (King David), and even sinful women can play important roles in God's kingdom (as when the prostitute Rahab hid Joshua's spies in the second chapter of Joshua).

Then there was the case when a group of scribes and Pharisees tried to catch Jesus off guard by bringing an unfaithful woman into His midst and watching to see if He would condemn her in accordance with Mosaic law. According to that law, they had a right to stone her to death for her sin of adultery: "Early in the morning he came again to the temple. All the people came to him, and he sat down and taught them. The scribes and the Pharisees brought a woman who had been caught in adultery, and placing her in the midst they said to him, 'Teacher, this woman has been caught in the act of adultery'" (John 8:2-4).

The story in John doesn't provide any background

information about the woman, but that didn't stop me from wondering about who she was and how she had wound up as an object lesson in a religious turf war between the Pharisees and Jesus.

For one thing, I wondered how she had been caught in the act of adultery. Did the Pharisees or their representatives actually barge into someone's house or room where the sexual sin was taking place? Had they planned their actions in conjunction with the man who was involved? And why didn't the Pharisees bring the man to Jesus instead of only bringing the woman?

The more I studied this passage, the more questions I had:

- What were this woman's thoughts and dreams?
- What was her life story? Where did she come from? And how did she get to this point?
- Was this woman being accused of adultery by someone who had a sinful past and a bad reputation?
- What sins had been committed against her?
- Was she in an abusive marriage and looking for a way out?
- Did she cry out to God or even believe in Him?
- Did she think her sins were too grave to be forgiven?
- Was she worried about being stoned to death for her sin?

I can't think of a more humiliating position for a woman to be in. This woman was thrown down before Jesus like a dirty rag, and all the crowd that had gathered around the scene looked to judge her.

I've been in the same situation in my own life. I had been unfaithful to Al. And the two of us had worked hard to redeem this situation and save our marriage. Knowing how complicated things can be, I decided I didn't want to prejudge Anna without hearing her side of the story, which was what Al and I set out to do later that Wednesday evening.

The Other Side of the Story

Anna came to our church office to meet us. The two of us had barely said hello to her before her story started spilling out:

"Over time," she said, "Trey and I gradually fell into a party lifestyle. We were going to clubs and drinking, and I was flirting a lot with other men just for fun. Trey enjoyed that.

"One day we were looking for a used car. We found one we liked, and when we were doing the paperwork with the salesman who had helped us, he began flirting with me in front of Trey. And then I flirted back. At the time, that wasn't considered unusual or inappropriate by either one of us.

"After we got the car home, we still had a few items to address about insurance. We decided I would be the one to relate to the salesman about anything we needed with the car. He and I would text back and forth to settle these issues. But pretty soon the texting started to include things that didn't have anything to do with our car.

"Two weeks after we drove that car home, the affair began. Trey only found out because I sent a sexy text to him by mistake when I meant to text the car salesman."

At this point, Anna abruptly stopped talking and started sobbing. It was like a dam holding back her feelings had broken, and now she started spilling out secrets she and Trey had been keeping well away from us and anyone else. Anna told us all the details, some of which we won't repeat here:

"Trey had gradually gotten back into viewing pornography, and now he wanted to bring porn into our marriage. He wanted me to watch porn with him before we would have sex. I never wanted pornography to be a part of our marriage, but I agreed to do it because I was so needy. I wanted to be the best wife in every way. I wanted him to just worship me. He told me that joining him in this practice would bring us closer together sexually and emotionally."

Anna took another break to catch her breath and blow her nose. "I thought the whole pornography thing would be enough for him, but the next thing I knew Trey was talking to me about us trying the 'swinging lifestyle.' He explained that couples will get together with other couples to exchange partners. I was hesitant about this, but Trey kept pressuring me, and finally I agreed, reluctantly.

"That's when we began searching for other couples online so we could swap partners with them. We would reach out to another couple online, and then we would meet at a motel for a few hours. Then we would never see that couple again.

"This happened three times. Trey seemed to enjoy it, but

I didn't. Before long, I just could not do it anymore. I felt dirty and sick every time we did this. Finally, I told Trey that I was done with swinging."

After more than an hour of conversation, Anna was completely broken. She said she felt devastated by everything she had been through, and she even apologized for having to tell us all about it.

Anna was dealing with some complex emotions. She was overcome with guilt about the affair with the car salesman, but she was also depressed about the pornography and the swinging that she and Trey had engaged in. Now it felt like she was being singled out and treated as the only sexual sinner by the man who had led her into infidelity.

It was late in the evening when we wrapped up our meeting.

"Anna," said Al, "we want to thank you for getting all of this out into the open with us. That was very brave. And I will make sure to get Trey's side of the story when I meet with him two days from now."

She wiped her eyes one final time and walked out the door. Next it would be Trey's time to talk.

Throwing Stones

After Trey came into Al's office and said hello, he laid out his case. Al didn't tell him about the things Anna had told us, and Trey didn't mention them either. Instead, Trey told his version of the events, focusing on his anger and disappointment with Anna.

"It all started a few days ago," Trey began. "I got a text from Anna that didn't make any sense at all. It said, 'I can't talk now. A neighbor is here.'

"I hadn't asked to talk to Anna, so I didn't text her back. I thought she meant it for someone else. But who? I was confused, but I didn't really have any reason to be suspicious of her.

"Then when I got home and opened the front door, Anna was standing there. She looked like she was about to burst. That's when she just spilled everything all out! She told me that she was having an affair with the car salesman. The text was supposed to go to him, not me. At first I thought she was joking. I basically trusted her. I just couldn't believe she would ever cheat on me. But this was no joke!"

Al listened as Trey told his story. Then he asked Trey how he felt about Anna's behavior.

"I'm *soooo* angry," he said. "This is all her fault!"

Al kept listening, hoping that Trey would gradually get around to how his own behavior had played a role in Anna's unfaithfulness. But he never mentioned pressuring Anna to view pornography and try swinging.

"So What Do You Say?"

After his meeting with Trey, Al told me about their conversation.

"Trey said the problem was all Anna," Al said. "He never said anything about the porn or the swinging."

I wasn't surprised.

Al and I were scheduled to meet with Trey and Anna together later in the week. Somehow, I had a feeling that this meeting between the four of us would bring out more truth from Trey. I knew that if Trey didn't volunteer the information, Al would gradually confront him with everything Anna had said and try to figure out who was telling the truth.

I could also see the parallels between what was happening with Trey and Anna and what had happened to the woman caught in adultery in the Gospel of John. Trey had reported on Anna's behavior, and he seemed to want Al and me to render judgment on Anna without letting the whole story be known.

I wondered if Jesus had similar doubts about male accusers when the Pharisees brought the woman into His presence and demanded that Jesus render judgment on her: "'Now in the Law, Moses commanded us to stone such women. So what do you say?' This they said to test him, that they might have some charge to bring against him. Jesus bent down and wrote with his finger on the ground" (John 8:5-6).

What was Jesus writing on the ground that day? We have wondered about that question many times. Was He writing a verse from the Hebrew Scriptures? Was He drawing a picture? We will never know.

Jesus had been confronted by the scribes and Pharisees, but it was pretty clear their agenda was about trapping Jesus, not making sure justice was done, and not caring about the sinful woman. These legalistic leaders were zealous followers of their version of God's law, and they taught that violators must be punished. But Jesus preached a message of love and grace and forgiveness. How would this confrontation end?

We didn't know how our meeting with Trey and Anna would end, but we prayed God's love and mercy would prevail.

The Words of Jesus Hit Home

We wanted to see how Trey would talk with Anna present. Would he remain prideful and blaming? Or would he recognize his own sin in the presence of the wife he had pressured to indulge in sexual sin with him? He certainly wasn't admitting any wrongdoing on his part or offering any grace to Anna beforehand.

The four of us met several days later, and we could see that Trey's pride and self-righteousness were still intact. We began to talk with Anna, who was crying and admitting her guilt and shame.

"I sat there and let that happen," Trey said.

When it was evident that Trey wasn't going to bring up his own sinful lifestyle, we told him that we knew all about it. He didn't defend himself by making excuses. He received the truth, and we began to see his pride slip away . . . just a little bit.

Trey admitted that he had brought Satan into his relationship with Anna from the beginning of their marriage with his use of pornography and then his desire for increased sexual excitement. He saw his need for deep change and began a journey in that direction. Trey knew he needed to receive God's grace, but his journey to being a grace-giver was long and difficult. Like the Pharisees, he repeatedly felt the urge to pick up stones and throw them at a woman who had sinned. And like the Pharisees, it was a lot easier for him to ignore his own failures if he just kept pointing to the failures of others. But he persevered in his arduous journey of grace.

A lot of Trey's actions had come out of his own hurt. Maybe some of the scribes and Pharisees John spoke about experienced the same thing: "As they continued to ask him, he stood up and said to them, 'Let him who is without sin among you be the first to throw a stone at her.' And once more he bent down and wrote on the ground. But when they heard it, they went away one by one, beginning with the older ones, and Jesus was left alone with the woman standing before him" (John 8:7-9).

This brief statement of Jesus stopped those men without any argument from them. They were speechless. They turned away.

When Al pointed out Trey's sin at that meeting, he stopped short too.

No Longer Condemned

Shortly after Anna had told us how she and Trey were living, she came to me (Al) and asked me to baptize her. I listened as she told me why.

"I've believed I was a Christian for twenty-eight years! But I see now that I wasn't. I saw being baptized as a way to stay out of hell. It was like checking a box of good things to do.

"I can't believe I've done so many terrible things. I'm so ashamed. That shame has torn me to pieces. I want to be baptized again as a sign that I've totally surrendered my life to Christ. No matter what, I'm serving the Lord from this point forward."

I baptized Anna the next night, and we saw the evident transformation in her whole being. When she came up out of the water, her hands were raised and she was smiling. She just shimmered with the glow of a redeemed life. We saw the surrender play out completely as she started to read the Bible and pray and hang on tight to Jesus. She began a journey that night that continues to this day.

As I (Lisa) watched Al baptize Anna, I wondered again about the woman standing before Jesus without any more accusers still there to condemn her: "Jesus stood up and said to her, 'Woman, where are they? Has no one condemned you?' She said, 'No one, Lord.' And Jesus said, 'Neither do I condemn you; go, and from now on sin no more'" (John 8:10-11).

What would she have done at that point? Did she grasp what had just happened when Jesus said, "Neither do I condemn you"? The desperate forgiveness she needed to free her from her guilt and shame was now hers if she would choose to accept it. I like to think she did accept it. Then her heart would have begun to heal, and her life, like Anna's, would have been transformed.

Trey Puts Down His Stones

Trey had admitted that he was the one who had brought Satan into their marriage, and Satan kept at him for a number of months to keep throwing stones at Anna by saying hurtful things and reminding her of her unfaithfulness to him.

He was still angry and wasn't meeting with us as frequently as Anna was. She was working on herself, and Trey was denying himself of the truth. He told us later how things finally began to change for him:

"I was all wrapped up in myself, and I wanted Anna to hurt. One day I went into the living room where she was sitting with her Bible open and her head bowed like she was praying. I accused her of just putting on a show. I kept saying things to get a fight started, but she didn't retaliate. That made me even madder, so I amped up my verbal attacks. I just wanted to have control over her, but she wouldn't respond. After several weeks of continual harassment, Anna moved in with her parents.

"Being alone finally caused me to start thinking about myself in honest ways. God started to remind me of my own sins and my need for repentance. That time alone with Him was a turning point for me. I admitted and confessed my sins to God and prayed for His mercy and forgiveness. I finally overcame sexual sin by understanding that His grace teaches us to say no to all types of ungodliness, and that His grace and forgiveness extended toward the horrible things I had done. It helped me to realize how much Jesus' death cost Him. I felt His forgiveness and then also felt His prodding to forgive Anna, as it says in Colossians 3:13-14: 'bearing with one another and, if one has a complaint against another, forgiving each other; as the Lord has forgiven you, so you also must forgive. And above all these put on love, which binds everything together in perfect harmony.'"

The Healing Power of Forgiveness

Trey and Anna got back together and began the journey of restoration. We saw them heal and grow and start to help others. When they saw someone hurting, they became spiritual first responders.

Like us, they began by telling their testimony after a few years of healing and growing. They were sponges for personal spiritual growth and also for marriage ministry. We witnessed their incredible transformation from a deeply troubled couple to a dynamic duo who helped other couples.

It is so evident that the forgiveness of God gave them the power to stay faithful to His Word. They are leaders in our church's marriage ministry, called "Reengage," and are continuing to help other struggling couples experience God's grace and mercy.

Trey and Anna have another important ministry in addition to their marriage work. They help men and women learn how to put down all the stones they want to pick up and throw at other sinners. Pharisees and other self-righteous people love throwing stones. What a great way to focus on the sins of *other people*! It's like the Canadian musician Bruce Cockburn sang:

Everybody
Loves to see
Justice done
On somebody else.[1]

Trey and Anna know better now. They know that forgiveness is a two-way street of "forgiving each other . . . as the Lord has forgiven you."

All of us have our judgmental moments when we want to come down hard on the failings of others, but that doesn't mean we must live our lives as Pharisees. The best thing you can do with all those rocks you want to throw is lay them down at the feet of Jesus as you ask Him to forgive *your* sins.

CHAPTER 8

TALES OF
THE FORGIVEN

FOR THE TWO OF US, the fall of 1999 was a dark and depressing season. Lisa had finally confessed to me (Al) about having an affair with another man, and we were separated as we tried to figure out what would happen next.

Lisa moved out of our house and began living with a friend while she waited to see what, if anything, would become of her now-broken marriage. She knew God had forgiven her, but she had less hope that I would ever forgive her and let her come back to me and the girls.

Meanwhile, I stayed in our home to serve as dad *and* mom for our daughters during this terrible time. By all appearances it seemed I was managing everything A-OK, but external appearances masked a major battle that I was fighting deep in my own soul. I knew what Lisa had done was wrong and hurtful and destructive, but what should I do now? I didn't have a clue. A sacred trust between us had been broken. Could it ever be restored?

Heartbroken, angry, and confused, I wrestled with the questions so many of us confront whenever people hurt us deep in our hearts:

Can I forgive her?

Should I forgive her?

I knew that Christ commands His followers to forgive those who sin against us. But how should I apply this biblical command in this situation? Could I ever really forgive Lisa for her sin and open my heart to her again? Right now, it seemed impossible that the two of us could ever restore our relationship and return to living as man and wife.

This was the sad situation we faced that fall. Our marriage was on life support. Our lives were in limbo. We prayed to God for help and guidance, but neither one of us felt as if we were getting clear responses to our petitions.

Thankfully, we both received a powerful message of love and grace from a man who had gone through many more trials and tribulations in life and marriage than we had ever experienced ourselves. His trauma and transformation helped each of us reorient our hearts to God's love, enabling us to heal our damaged souls.

The lessons we learned about guilt and forgiveness saved our threatened marriage and enabled us to trust and love each other fully once again. We want to share these life-changing lessons with you.

Suddenly It Was Clear!

"Al, you must read this book," a friend told me as he handed me a copy of *Getting Past Guilt* by a man named Joe Beam. "I think this will really help you in your situation."

I was desperate for help, but I was also skeptical that any one book could address the many feelings and challenges that were raging within my heart. I accepted the gift and decided I would read it during a long flight to Germany, where I was scheduled to preach.

So many times when we find ourselves in horrible predicaments, we mistakenly conclude that our situation is totally unique or that the crises in our lives are much, much worse than anything anyone else has ever confronted. It's ridiculous how often we do this to ourselves, but that's exactly how I felt during this time of separation from Lisa.

But as soon as I opened Joe's book and read a bit of his story, I knew I was hearing from someone who had been through more pain and torment than I had. After reading the first few pages, I realized this book would be both moving and disturbing. That's why I decided to stop reading. After all, I was on my way to preach to people about the love of God. I was afraid if I read any more of this book, I would be so emotional and vulnerable that I might not be able to preach effectively and help the people who were waiting for me.

So I did something pastors, preachers, and many others among us often do: I compartmentalized. I told myself, *Okay, these nice people in Germany aren't flying me all the way to Europe so I can have a public breakdown. They've invited me to reach people for Christ. So let's focus on that mission for now, and I can always have my own personal breakdown later!*

In a few days, I was on my way back to the United States on another long plane flight. During that flight I read the entire book from cover to cover. By the time I finished chapter 6, suddenly it was clear! I knew what I needed to do. I needed to forgive Lisa. I needed to give our love another chance.

This revelation came from Joe Beam's story about a deacon in his church named Bobby.

Bobby's Burden

The thirty-five-year-old man who had requested the meeting walked into the pastor's study at the small church in LaGrange, Georgia.

Joe asked how he could help, and Bobby told him he'd been struggling with guilt for fifteen years over a willful sin he had committed. He had prayed about it at length, asked for forgiveness, and studied it in the Bible. He had asked his wife to pray about it too, but he still felt guilty.

Joe asked about the sin, wondering what could cause so much guilt. He thought it might be infidelity, alcohol or drug abuse, or some sort of violent crime.

Bobby confessed that when he had been in the Army

fifteen years before, stationed in Germany, he hadn't gone to church regularly. In fact, he had only gone a few times during the whole year.

"And what else?" Joe asked, assuming there must be something else more serious.

Bobby stared at the pastor, thinking the man of God had lost his mind. That was it: he hadn't gone to church, and it was still eating him up inside. He needed help.

At the time Joe was only a green, twenty-two-year-old pastor, but he responded with the wisdom of a mature mind, framing his response in the form of a parable:

Bobby, suppose that one morning before you left for work you asked your ten-year-old son, Jeff, to feed the dogs. But when you got home, you realized they hadn't been fed. So you talked to Jeff about what happened.

Then suppose that Jeff apologized to you for his oversight, begged for forgiveness, and immediately went off to feed the dogs. So far, so good.

But the next day, when you came home from work, you saw Jeff sitting alone under a tree. When you asked Jeff why he was all alone under the tree, your son confessed.

"Dad, I feel so guilty about not feeding the dogs yesterday. It's really bugging me."

Bobby, what would you say to your son at that point? I suspect it might be something like this:

"Son, that whole problem is over and done with. You apologized and asked for my forgiveness. I forgave you. You fed the dogs. Everything is settled and resolved."

Now, Bobby, let's fast-forward a bit. Jeff is now eighteen and is graduating from high school. But right after he receives his diploma, he comes to you and tells you how upset he is about the dog-feeding incident from eight years earlier. How would you respond to that? Wouldn't you tell him that the whole episode was over and done with?

Now, fast-forward again. Jeff has just gotten married, and at the reception, he tells you how upset he is about the dog-feeding incident from fifteen years earlier. Wouldn't you think that was going overboard?

Somehow that parable woke Bobby up to the fact that he had needlessly spent the last fifteen years of his life feeling guilty about his horrible record of church attendance in Germany. He realized this was something God had forgiven the *first* time he begged for God's forgiveness.[1]

Somehow, the parable hit me upside the head too. I couldn't explain why this one simple story impacted me so deeply, but I knew as soon as I had read it that it spoke to the problem that Lisa and I were facing.

Lisa had apologized and asked forgiveness from God and

from me. Now I realized I would need to forgive Lisa, no matter how uncomfortable and vulnerable that felt.

Meanwhile, Lisa had been reading her own copy of *Getting Past Guilt*, and it was having an impact on her, too.

Who Was That Person?

A strange thing happened to me (Lisa) during that long and difficult night when I confessed all my sins and unfaithfulness to Al. After hours of confession and answering all of Al's questions, I remember thinking:

Who is this person who just confessed all this horrible sin?

And why in the world would this person ever do all of these sinful acts?

Al was the one person in the world I never wanted to hurt, but I had hurt him deeply. How could I do that to him?

What made me do all these things?

It was strange to observe myself as if I was another person, but when I sat back and looked at all my deceptive and destructive behaviors, I really didn't like myself very much. I began to see my sin for what it was, and it was ugly.

Who is this deceptive and despicable person I have been describing all these hours?

Is this lying and deceiving person who I really am deep down?

What was it within me that made all of this happen?

After studying Scripture and reading Joe's book, I could see things more clearly. I didn't realize it at the time, but Satan had won over my heart, my mind, and my body. Now

I wanted to better understand the process the enemy used to trip me up.

As I was reading the Bible a short time later, I could see that the questions I was asking myself covered some of the same problems Paul explored in his letter to the Christians in Rome:

> For I do not understand my own actions. For I do
> not do what I want, but I do the very thing I hate.
> Now if I do what I do not want, I agree with the
> law, that it is good. So now it is no longer I who
> do it, but sin that dwells within me. For I know
> that nothing good dwells in me, that is, in my
> flesh. For I have the desire to do what is right, but
> not the ability to carry it out. For I do not do the
> good I want, but the evil I do not want is what I
> keep on doing. Now if I do what I do not want,
> it is no longer I who do it, but sin that dwells
> within me.
>
> ROMANS 7:15-20

It seemed that Paul had put on X-ray goggles and was looking deep into the darkness of my soul. Like Paul said, I didn't understand my own actions. I hadn't done what I wanted, but instead I did the very thing I didn't want to do: hurt Al. I had the desire to do what was right but not the ability to carry it out. Sin was dwelling within me.

I was suddenly overwhelmed with the gravity of my

situation. For a moment, I thought, *I'm just going to die all alone right here, with nobody beside me, because of my selfishness and sin.* I was desperate for God's forgiveness—more desperate than I have ever been—because I could clearly see my sin revealed in the light of God's love.

The whole experience was incredibly painful but also transforming. I came away with a better understanding of how complicated things are deep inside of me and underneath the surface I present to the world.

I wasn't sure if Al would ever forgive me. But if he did, I didn't ever want to hurt him again, so I asked God to help me go back in time and see exactly how I had given in to temptation so willingly. I also started seeing a Christian counselor, and I told her that one of her assignments was helping me understand how I had fallen so far.

I wanted to understand sin from beginning to end. Before, I had understood sin as particular bad actions or wrongful behaviors, such as marital unfaithfulness. But now I understood sin in a broader way. I came to see how our enemy uses all of our desires, temptations, and carelessness to plant seeds of disobedience in our hearts. Then we water that seed of sin and bring it to action instead of turning our backs on it.

A Golden Boy Gone Bad

The man who wrote *Getting Past Guilt* faced some of the same sins we faced in our own marriage.

Joe was a golden boy: smart, attractive, and well spoken.

Called to the ministry at a young age, Joe was a so-so pastor, but he was a great preacher. By the time he was twenty-four years old, he had already become a star of the traveling revival circuit. Joe told us what he had gone through:

> When a famous evangelist who was scheduled
> to speak to two thousand teenagers at a big rally
> in Tuscaloosa, Alabama, needed to cancel at the
> last minute, he told the organizers to call me so I
> could replace him. That was my big break. After
> that, churches all over the Southeast began calling
> me to speak at their revivals. By the time I was
> thirty, I was speaking at revivals here, there, and
> everywhere. So many churches wanted me to
> speak that I was booking events six years out.
>
> At one revival, a major church leader came up to
> me and told me that I was "a shining star arising on
> the brotherhood's horizon." Unfortunately, I totally
> believed him, and I started thinking of myself as a
> Talented Young Preacher. That was the beginning
> of the end for me.
>
> The proverb warns that "pride goes before
> destruction, and a haughty spirit before a fall"
> (Proverbs 16:18). I was pumped full of pride,
> and when I fell, I fell hard.
>
> The occasion of my fall was a big debate in our
> church about grace and judgment. My sermons
> on God's grace generated heavy criticism. I would

get telephone calls and letters every day claiming that I was a false teacher who was going to hell. They claimed I was preaching that sin didn't matter (which wasn't true). They said I was preaching that grace was all that mattered (which wasn't true).

As the accusations flew my way, all my future preaching engagements were abruptly canceled. I felt I was coming under intense pressure. It seemed like it was me against the world. I was desperate for support and affirmation.

Meanwhile, my wife, Alice, was getting anxious about our family's financial future.

"I think you need to back off from all this teaching," she told me.

I desperately needed Alice to stand with me in my valiant battle for God, the Bible, and everything true. I needed her beside me in my battle against Pharisees in the church. Suddenly, it seemed she had turned against me. Now I felt totally alone. In my mind, Alice had become part of the big, bad world that was out to get me.

That was when a single woman came to see me at the church for pastoral counseling. Perhaps you can see where this is heading? Over the course of numerous counseling sessions, I developed an emotional relationship with her. Before long I had concluded, "No one understands me . . . except her!"

Our emotional connection gradually turned into a sexual affair. I did all I could to hide our relationship from church members, but then a member who saw the two of us sneaking off for a clandestine rendezvous reported us to the church elders. The church fired me. I was thirty-four years old.

You might think this sudden change of fortune would bring me to my senses, but it didn't. This golden-throated preacher boy still had farther to fall.

Things continued to go downhill for me.

After the church fired me, I moved out of town.

Within the year, Alice and I divorced.

My relationship with the single woman ended.

I started a business, but it failed, and I went bankrupt.

I began abusing alcohol and drugs, and I spent my nights hanging out in disreputable dive bars.

I learned to tell jokes to people in the hopes that they would buy me a drink. I was trying this routine one night when the man sitting next to me in the bar leaned over and said, "You know, I always thought you were the best preacher I ever heard."

One night I overdosed on too much alcohol and too many drugs. I was rushed to the emergency room, but not even that scare was enough to slow my descent into a cesspool of sin.

It would require a second trip to the emergency room, where this time I almost died, and a doctor had to pump my stomach. The next day, as I was recovering, the intensive care nurse had a question for me:

"Did you mean to kill yourself?"

"I was just trying not to hurt," I answered. "I don't want to hurt anymore."

That was my lowest point. It was finally my time for desperate forgiveness. Right then I turned to God and said, "This is not the way I want to die. Show me how to live and die the right way."

After much prayer and struggle, Alice forgave me and welcomed me back, promising never to use my sins against me in the future. More than thirty years later, we are still together, and she has never used my past mistakes to hurt me.

Today, Alice and I lead weekend marriage retreats for couples in crisis with our ministry, Marriage Helper (MarriageHelper.com). Two-thirds of the couples who come to us for help are dealing with issues of infidelity, and we are grateful that the experiences we have had on our journey can help them on their journeys. And because our story helped Al and Lisa heal their marriage, they now serve on the Marriage Helper advisory board.

Not everyone comes to a place as desperate as mine was, but no matter what it is you've done, God's grace is sufficient if you will repent and seek His forgiveness.[2]

Finally Desperate Enough for Forgiveness?
What's the difference between people who are desperate for forgiveness and people who haven't yet reached their point of desperation?

We think the major difference is pretty simple:

- Some of us have come to a place where we know what it is to hunger and thirst for Christ's love and forgiveness more than anything else in the world.

- Others aren't yet desperate enough, and they continue to cling to all the other things they desire, need, or love more than forgiveness.

Jesus met both kinds of people during His ministry years, and the different ways He engaged with them makes it obvious who was desperate and who wasn't. Two stories from the Gospels make this distinction crystal clear.

Story 1: The Golden Boy Who Wasn't Desperate Enough
We think of Joe Beam every time we read the story in the Gospels where Jesus meets that era's version of the golden boy. This man was wealthy and powerful. He seemed to have nearly everything going for him. This golden boy said he wanted eternal life, but he apparently didn't want it enough:

And behold, a man came up to him, saying, "Teacher, what good deed must I do to have eternal life?" And he said to him, "Why do you ask me about what is good? There is only one who is good. If you would enter life, keep the commandments." He said to him, "Which ones?" And Jesus said, "You shall not murder, You shall not commit adultery, You shall not steal, You shall not bear false witness, Honor your father and mother, and, You shall love your neighbor as yourself." The young man said to him, "All these I have kept. What do I still lack?" Jesus said to him, "If you would be perfect, go, sell what you possess and give to the poor, and you will have treasure in heaven; and come, follow me." When the young man heard this he went away sorrowful, for he had great possessions.

And Jesus said to his disciples, "Truly, I say to you, only with difficulty will a rich person enter the kingdom of heaven. Again I tell you, it is easier for a camel to go through the eye of a needle than for a rich person to enter the kingdom of God." When the disciples heard this, they were greatly astonished, saying, "Who then can be saved?" But Jesus looked at them and said, "With man this is impossible, but with God all things are possible."

MATTHEW 19:16-26

Matthew tells us the juicy details about this man: he was rich, he was a ruler, and he was an avid law keeper. Was he good-looking? We'll never know for sure, but we suspect he was, and he was probably charming as well.

When we teach about this passage, we ask our listeners to picture this man. He's the kind of guy who made others jealous because they wanted to be him; the kind of guy dads wanted their daughter to marry; the kind of guy who was always being recruited to lead projects and manage people.

This young man was seeking perfection, goodness, and eternal life. So why did he walk away from the one person who could give him all three? The answer is pretty simple.

This man walked away from Jesus because he loved something more than he loved God. Maybe it was the money he loved more. Maybe it was being able to run his own life the way he wanted without someone else telling him what he should do.

Whatever it was that held him back, this man clung to it for all he was worth.

Christ's grace can wash away any sin, but forgiveness only comes to us when we give up whatever it is that holds us back from Christ. Christ loves everyone, and He asks each one of us to love Him more than we love everything else.

Who then can be saved? For the rich young man, forgiveness proved too costly. But for one other man Jesus met, no price was too high to pay for the gift of God's forgiveness.

Story 2: The Man Who Demonstrated His Desperation
A different Gospel story shows a different outcome:

[Jesus] entered Jericho and was passing through. And behold, there was a man named Zacchaeus. He was a chief tax collector and was rich. And he was seeking to see who Jesus was, but on account of the crowd he could not, because he was small in stature. So he ran on ahead and climbed up into a sycamore tree to see him, for he was about to pass that way. And when Jesus came to the place, he looked up and said to him, "Zacchaeus, hurry and come down, for I must stay at your house today." So he hurried and came down and received him joyfully. And when they saw it, they all grumbled, "He has gone in to be the guest of a man who is a sinner." And Zacchaeus stood and said to the Lord, "Behold, Lord, the half of my goods I give to the poor. And if I have defrauded anyone of anything, I restore it fourfold." And Jesus said to him, "Today salvation has come to this house, since he also is a son of Abraham. For the Son of Man came to seek and to save the lost."

LUKE 19:1-10

Here's how we picture Zacchaeus: short, probably bald, probably fat, and possibly sporting a big, bulbous nose. He was far from being a golden boy, and it was more likely he was loathed by Jews who were forced to pay him tax money to support the Roman occupation of Jewish lands.

But even with all these problems, Zacchaeus had this

much going for him: he had a hunger for forgiveness, and he was totally excited about seeing Jesus—so excited he clumsily forced his large frame to climb a tree so he could get a better look at his Savior. Can you imagine how this ridiculous behavior looked to his wife, his kids, or his neighbors?

When Jesus looked at him and called out to him, Zacchaeus didn't need to stop and weigh his options. He hurried down the tree and joyfully welcomed Jesus into his home. Zacchaeus fell in love with Jesus, and he loved Jesus more than he loved anything else, including money.

"Today salvation has come to this house," Jesus said, "for the Son of Man came to seek and to save the lost."

From Unforgiven to Forgiven

You would not believe some of the mind-boggling stories people tell us when we speak to groups about desperate forgiveness.

Some people are in situations similar to the one Al faced, asking themselves:

Can I forgive her?

Should I forgive her?

We're so thankful Al made the right call by doing what Jesus tells all of us to do in His most famous prayer, when He says, "and forgive us our debts, as we also have forgiven our debtors" (Matthew 6:12). Al opened the door for God's forgiveness to restore our broken marriage, and His grace is still flowing through our lives today.

Some people are in the same situation as Bobby, who

worried for fifteen years that God hadn't forgiven him. Because of Lisa's openness to talk about her abortion, many women come to us weighed down after wrestling with guilt for decades over an abortion they had in high school or college. We even hear from a few men who feel guilty over pressuring their girlfriends to get abortions.

What a joy it is to pray with these people who have been tormented by years' worth of guilt or unforgiven sin.

"The only person preventing you from being forgiven is *you*," we tell them. "So if you're ready to stop clinging to your own sin, if you're ready to repent and lay your burdens down at Jesus' feet, let's pray together and seek His forgiveness."

Thanks to God's grace, all the stories in this chapter turned out well—except for one. These people experienced forgiveness when they were desperate for it:

Al forgave Lisa.

God forgave Bobby.

Alice forgave Joe.

And Jesus forgave Zacchaeus.

Only one story didn't turn out too well. Remember our rich, young golden boy? Jesus challenged the man to give away half of his fortune, but that was too big a price for him to pay. The man went away sorrowful.

We don't want you to go away sorrowful. Don't carry your burden any longer. If you're finally desperate enough, seek God's forgiveness with all your heart.

CHAPTER 9

CHOOSE FORGIVENESS, NOT DESPAIR

BRANDON BAILEY WAS A PILLAR OF THE community around our hometown of West Monroe, Louisiana.

He was a respected businessman who was known throughout the community for networking and being involved in local groups. He was a loyal member of his church, serving on the elder board and teaching Sunday school classes. He was a good father and husband who loved his family and helped raise his children. He was also a good personal friend of our family, and he helped us out in many ways.

Brandon was a good guy who always had a smile on his face. He was the kind of guy everyone believed had it all together, someone who worked to make the world a much better place.

That's why it was so shocking for all of us when one day he walked out behind his house and shot himself in the head.

All we had left now were questions:

Why did he do it? Why did he end his life?

What private issues had been eating at him?

Why didn't he talk to one of the many people who loved him and cared for him before taking this desperate action?

Had all of us been fooled about who Brandon was and what he was doing with his life?

Shocked Survivors

We were shocked when Brandon left this world. (We have changed his name to protect his family.) How could a man who seemingly had it all together do this? We also wondered what secrets would be revealed as time went on. Often, we don't really know people as well as we think we do. We don't know their personal struggles, their hidden pain, their pressing burdens. Often, we only know what people allow us to see.

Apparently, Brandon had been experiencing financial difficulties for some time, even though he gave the impression that he was on top of his game. He was trying to maintain a luxurious lifestyle when he really didn't have the income.

Brandon had been hiding behind a big mask. Wearing masks can be fun if you're going to a costume party or you're playing a special role in a play, but hiding behind a mask is a horrible way to live your life. Brandon might have feared that when people knew he was broke, they wouldn't want to be his friend. And maybe he wondered if his family would love him after his mask came off.

The Desperation of Despair

Throughout this book we have looked at people whose lives are examples of desperate forgiveness. In these cases, the desperation people experienced led them to seek God's help and forgiveness. That's why we see desperate forgiveness as the start of a new chapter.

But in Brandon's case, desperation simply led to more desperation. And as his financial and emotional life went quickly downhill, he gave in to that desperation, ending his life, apparently because he didn't think anything could be done to fix his troubles.

Isn't that the way sin works? It makes us desperate and alone, craving fellowship with others, yet unwilling to relinquish our hold upon the hurt and pain that consume our existence. Sin makes us desperate. Desperate to find the next thing that will alleviate the guilt or that next relationship that will take our minds off our loneliness, just as long as it doesn't shine the light of truth upon what we know is wrong in our own lives.

But there *is* a way out of desperation. Nearly everyone experiences some form of despair during life's difficult seasons. Our plea to you is simple: Don't stay there. Don't make yourself so comfortable with despair that it becomes a major, recurring theme of your life.

We've seen that desperation can lead people in two completely different directions:

1. to significant change and repentance, and to the experience of forgiveness, freedom, and God's grace; or,
2. to more despair, frustration, and bitterness—and even to suicide.

You *can* find a way out of your desperate situation, and your way out doesn't have to be suicide.

Suicide Nation

Sadly, Brandon's case isn't unique. According to the Centers for Disease Control and Prevention, nearly forty-five thousand Americans killed themselves in 2016.[1]

We've seen this terrible toll ourselves, and not only in the case of Brandon. Al has been involved in the funerals of hundreds of people, and a few of these were suicides. Funerals are already horribly sad for some family members and loved ones, but they are a lot more difficult when suicide is the cause of death.

Recently, Al preached at the funeral for his fifty-two-year-old first cousin, who committed suicide in a jail cell. He had been addicted to opioids for fifteen years, and his addiction led him down a trail of betrayal and belligerence toward almost everyone in the family. Apparently he reached his point of desperation in that jail cell, deciding that he would never be able to straighten out his life and that nobody would really miss him when he was gone. He was wrong about that.

Over the years, several members of Lisa's extended family have also attempted suicide after dealing with addiction, depression, and mental illness.

Even one of Jesus' disciples ended his own life.

Desperate Views

Brandon Bailey's death came nearly two thousand years after Judas the disciple of Jesus died by his own hand. Brandon and Judas lived centuries apart, but they shared a desperate view of the world. Ultimately, both felt trapped, as if there was no way out of the difficult predicaments they had created around themselves.

Brandon and Judas are only two members of a very large group: desperate people who, for reasons only they understood, made a fateful choice. They chose not to lay their burdens at the feet of Christ, who could forgive and heal their sins. They instead chose to deal with life's problems by ending their lives.

Judas was one of Jesus' original twelve disciples, but he turned against his Lord. That must have hurt Jesus, to see His friend turn against Him like that.

The Gospel of Matthew records the suicide in this brief report:

Then when Judas, his betrayer, saw that Jesus was condemned, he changed his mind and brought back the thirty pieces of silver to the chief priests and the elders, saying, "I have sinned by betraying innocent blood." They said, "What is that to us? See to it yourself." And throwing down the pieces of silver into the temple, he departed, and he went and hanged himself.

MATTHEW 27:3-5

We wonder if Judas thought the way many suicidal people probably do: *I've gone and messed up everything, and now there's nothing left for me to do but to end it all.*

It was after Jesus was condemned that Judas had second thoughts about turning Him in. But by then it was too late to reverse the chain of events. Soon, Jesus would be abused and crucified. That's when Judas saw only one way out: suicide.

Why Suicide?

People with major psychiatric illness or mood disorders are at risk for suicide. Other at-risk groups include adolescents and young men twenty-four years old and under, men over the age of eighty, prison inmates, LGBT youth and adults, certain minority groups (including Native Americans), and people with prior histories of attempted suicide or a family history of suicide.

But suicide also stalks people like Brandon Bailey, who are not part of these at-risk groups. Mental health experts say these are typical causes:

- Substance abuse or misuse, especially with alcohol
- Strained or broken relationships with family, friends, or other loved ones
- Major life losses, such as the death of a loved one; the loss of a job or professional honor; or other significant losses, including income, health, and social networks
- Crying out for help—some people kill themselves because they feel no one cares about them or loves them
- Experiencing seemingly unbearable emotional or physical pain
- Childhood trauma, including bullying, emotional or sexual abuse, serious family dysfunction, or time spent in foster care
- Big mistakes—for example, losing money in risky investments, blowing a big job interview, or plowing a car into several neighbors' cars during a drunken rage
- An impulsive decision—it's not uncommon for teenagers to kill themselves after a boyfriend or girlfriend has broken up with them
- A problem with gambling

As we look at this list of troublesome items, we can check off those challenges we have struggled with in our own lives.

Substance abuse or misuse? Check.
Strained or broken relationships? Check.
Major life losses? Check.

Enduring emotional or physical pain? Check.

Childhood trauma? Check.

Big mistakes and impulsive decisions? Double check.

In our lives, we have made many bad choices and destructive decisions that hurt ourselves and the people around us. There have been times when we felt depressed and thought, *This world and everyone in it would be a lot better off without me!*

But thanks to our connections to God and our loved ones, our sadness and sorrows didn't spiral downward to deadly despair and death. We believe that strengthening these loving connections can provide an emotional safety net that keeps people from falling into the pit of despair.

No Perfect People

In June 2018, suicide was headline news:

- Celebrated designer Kate Spade, fifty-five, committed suicide on June 5.
- Popular TV tour guide Anthony Bourdain, sixty-one, killed himself on June 8.
- A few days later, the Centers for Disease Control and Prevention announced that rates of death by suicide in the United States had risen more than 30 percent in almost half the states between 1999 and 2016.[2]

We've heard people say that celebrity suicides don't make any sense. "How could someone who has everything, including fame and fortune, be that depressed?" they ask. But such thinking reveals our infatuation with the myth of celebrity. We assume that famous, well-paid celebrities live wonderful, glamorous lives with little pain or loss. Unfortunately, not even fame can insulate us from the hard things that are part of everyday life.

There's a deeper problem all of us must face, no matter what our status in life. Psychology professor Clay Routledge wrote that that deeper problem is a crisis of meaninglessness that cuts across all differences in wealth and status: "I am convinced that our nation's suicide crisis is in part a crisis of meaninglessness. . . . A felt lack of meaning in one's life has been linked to alcohol and drug abuse, depression, anxiety, and—yes—suicide. And when people experience loss, stress, or trauma, it is those who believe that their lives have a purpose who are best able to cope with and recover from distress."[3]

Routledge said that a sense of meaning and purpose in life comes from people and things outside of ourselves. The biggest source of meaning? Deep relationships that can help people cope with the stresses they experience in life. Superficial relationships aren't strong enough to help. "Merely pleasant or enjoyable social encounters aren't enough to stave off despair," wrote Routledge.[4]

God created us to love Him and to love our neighbors, and we've seen that loving relationships with God and other people are a key to finding meaning and purpose in life.

You may be struggling to relate to some of the people in

your life, but you need deep relationships with others to survive and thrive. Seek out relationships where you and others can forge deep bonds of love and trust. And try thinking about others more than you think about yourself.

Perhaps you feel you are struggling in your relationship with God. Brandon Bailey apparently struggled to love God and be loved by God, even though he put on a good front at church. We all need God's love in our lives at least as much as we need food, water, and air. Don't let guilt or shame prevent you from bringing your sorrows and sins to Christ, asking for His forgiveness, and longing to experience His love.

At times it may seem that celebrity, wealth, and power are what one needs in life. But love is more powerful than all these things. Seek love and you will find life—the most powerful antidote to despair.

The Unforgivable Sin?

When Al is the pastor officiating at a funeral for a Christian who died by suicide, people always ask us, "Will God forgive this sin?" We've even heard some believers call suicide the unforgivable sin, even though the Bible never calls it that.

There are about half a dozen cases of suicide in the Bible, but none of them are condemned outright. Samson killed himself in the process of attacking a pagan temple and was praised for his bravery.

Some people argue that suicide *can't* be forgiven because people who kill themselves die without repenting or seeking forgiveness. But all of us will be in big trouble if God demands we confess *all* our sins by the moment we die. We feel this is a legalistic way of looking at sin and grace that discounts what it means to live in Christ.

We've also heard people argue that those who kill themselves are technically insane when they end their lives, but we don't think that's necessarily the case. Some people rationally commit suicide after months or years of planning and preparation.

If the Bible does not condemn these tortured souls, neither will we. God's ways are mysterious, but we hope and pray that He will extend His grace and forgiveness in death to those who did not experience it in life.

A writer for *Christianity Today* expressed this hope when answering a reader who had asked the question "What is the biblical hope and comfort we can offer a suicide victim's family and friends?"

The answer was comforting: "Will Jesus welcome home a believer who died at her own hands? I believe he will, tenderly and lovingly. My biblical basis? It is the hope-giving promise . . . that neither life nor death can separate the believer from the love of God in Christ Jesus."[5] (See Romans 8:38-39.)

When Al was preparing his sermon for his first cousin's funeral, he knew there were some in the family who believed suicide is unforgivable, but he still offered a message of hope and forgiveness. Al urged all present to forgive the cousin. That wouldn't be easy, because most of the people at that funeral had been hurt, swindled, or betrayed by this tortured man. But Al said it was important to forgive past hurts and sins instead of letting bitterness build and build.

"He didn't have an opportunity to make things right with all of us in this life," Al said, "but we still have the opportunity to forgive him."

There were a few calls of "Amen!" and many tears that day as brokenhearted people released the burden of sin's awful weight and sought to forgive one conflicted soul.

Choose Life

History is full of cases where people chose death rather than facing other choices they considered more horrible, but none of this explains why a beloved man like Brandon Bailey would take his own life.

Since Brandon's death, we've tried to be more sensitive to the fact that people we know and see every day of our lives may be struggling with monumental life challenges or wrestling in the depths of despair. We're not sure why people would rather disappear than embrace God's love and forgiveness, but we've learned to watch out for some of the suicide warning signs.

Is someone you know:

- exhibiting signs of depression, or significant sadness and hopelessness?
- gaining or losing weight, losing their appetite, finding it hard to sleep, or undergoing other major or sudden physical changes?

- withdrawing from the world, family, loved ones, friends, or people at church to whom they were previously close?
- expressing doubts about their inherent worth or value to others?
- talking about death, suicide, or "getting their affairs in order"?

After Brandon Bailey took his life, hundreds of people who were part of his family, or who knew him from his work in the community, or who worshipped with him every Sunday at church, were shocked and saddened by his sudden death. Everyone who knew and loved Brandon mourned his loss, including Al, who had been Brandon's pastor for many years. For months, Al wrestled with what he could have done to reach out to Brandon while he was alive. But after a while, Al decided to turn his grief into action by placing a greater emphasis on forgiveness in his preaching and teaching.

"You can't choose who your parents are or what they do to you," says Al. "You can't always control what happens to you in life. But there's one thing that is up to you. You can choose life instead of death. You can choose love instead of isolation or hate. You can choose forgiveness instead of hatred, anger, guilt, and shame.

"Your life may not be perfect, but life is God's gift to you. You can make the most of what you have by choosing life over death, loving God, and loving your neighbor.

"And if you are struggling with desperation that feels deadly, please reach out and share your pain with someone who loves you."

Get Support

If you are having thoughts of suicide, please call the National Suicide Prevention Lifeline at 1-800-273-TALK (8255).

CHAPTER 10

GENERATIONAL CURSES AND FORGIVENESS

I (LISA) NEVER TOLD ANYONE I WAS sexually abused as a child until decades later. My abuser told me that if I did tell anyone, I would get in a lot of trouble. You've already read in previous chapters how burying that abuse damaged my thinking about myself and contributed to some very poor choices.

What I hadn't known was that my silence also kept a generational sin in our family from being exposed and dealt with. When I finally told my mother about it, she told me that another relative had also sexually abused her.

There are several ways that the phrase "generational curses" may be defined. For our purposes here, we will use the following definition that Al and I consider our brief, summarized meaning: generational curses are those sinful attitudes and behaviors that negatively impact family members and may be passed down through generations if not recognized and resolved.

My mother kept her abuse a secret in her heart and buried her feelings. Buried feelings don't go away just because we keep trying to banish the thoughts of the pain we carry. Other emotions and behaviors rise up out of that pain and refuse to remain quiet. Anger, shame, verbal abuse, alcoholism, drug use, physical abuse, sexual abuse, and a host of other harmful attitudes and behaviors manifest themselves in many families and are often present in families living with generational curses. My mother kept her secret and, as a result, she carried shame and anger most of her life. Her family, including me, suffered with her.

So, what do generational curses have to do with forgiveness?

We are called to forgive others. But doesn't it seem reasonable to withhold forgiveness from someone who has hurt us? Why should we forgive such terrible treatment? The following verse gives part of the answer to that question: "See to it that no one fails to obtain the grace of God; that no 'root of bitterness' springs up and causes trouble" (Hebrews 12:15).

While it may seem reasonable to withhold forgiveness from people who hurt us, we will be the ones suffering for it. Unforgiveness nourishes a root of bitterness. That root grows and can strangle good growth inside of us. And trouble is the result: trouble for ourselves, and trouble for our families in the form of dysfunctional and fractured relationships and continuing generational curses.

We are to forgive people who hurt us because doing so is godly, and it is good for us. It frees us from reliving the pain we have suffered, from filling our minds with negativity that may cause discouragement, and from low self-esteem and depression. It allows us to experience the love and comfort of God.

Remember what we've already said in previous chapters: *forgiveness does not necessarily mean reconciliation.* I have forgiven my abuser, but I am not in relationship with him. I am blessed with the benefits just mentioned because I chose forgiveness. And I continue to protect my emotions by distancing myself from him.

Now we'll take a look at the impact of generational curses on my mother and me and consider a biblical story that dramatically shows how forgiveness from the impact of generational curses changed a family's destiny. Then you'll read how to address generational curses and find desperate forgiveness in your family.

Generational Sin in My Family

My mother and I both suffered the generational sins of unresolved sexual abuse and conditional love. My mother's coping mechanism was to try to keep up the image of a perfect family. My coping mechanism was to try to please the men in my life.

As a little girl, I had no idea how the ongoing abuse was weaving its way into my thinking and my choices. And that impact didn't show up until I was a teenager. My mother and I had a sweet relationship until then. I remember sitting in her lap in a recliner with my dad in another one next to us. We would be watching television after supper, and it felt safe and loving. My older brother and sister would sit on the floor in front of us. We were the image of a "normal" family.

Then I hit my teen years, and hormones converged with poor self-esteem. The poor self-esteem came from the damage of sexual abuse telling me that I was on earth to please men and boys. The hormones were evidence of the normal development of a young woman.

I would stay out late and sometimes skip school. It was wrong, and my mother would attempt to ground me. But because I was a daddy's girl, I convinced my father to overrule my mom and lift the grounding punishments. This would infuriate my mother, and she and Daddy would fight about my manipulative behavior. I know now that this wasn't the way to parent a rebellious teen, but I took full advantage of it.

My mother would withdraw her loving attitude from me when I disobeyed her and would seem to withdraw her actual love for me as well. In her life, she had learned that love was conditional: if you obeyed, you were loved; if you disobeyed, you were not loved. So that's how she related to me.

By the time I got pregnant, my mother had been trying for years to keep up the appearance of a perfect family. Her teenage daughter having a baby was simply not allowable. I'm not sure she ever considered the alternative of my giving birth to the baby. It was all such a shaming mess to her.

Generational Sin in Joseph's Family

The sins of generational deceit show up in the biblical story of Joseph and how he ended up in Egypt as a young man.

> Now his brothers went to pasture their father's flock near Shechem. And Israel said to Joseph, "Are not your brothers pasturing the flock at Shechem? Come, I will send you to them." And he said to him, "Here I am." So he said to him, "Go now, see if it is well with your brothers and with the flock, and bring me word." So he sent him from the Valley of Hebron, and he came to Shechem. And a man found him wandering in the fields. And the man asked him, "What are you seeking?" "I am seeking my brothers," he said. "Tell me, please, where they are pasturing the flock." And the man said, "They have gone away, for I heard them say, 'Let us go to Dothan.'" So Joseph went after his brothers and found them at Dothan.
>
> GENESIS 37:12-17

In the verses leading up to this passage, we read that a number of things had happened that caused Joseph's brothers to hate him.

- He had given a bad report of his brothers to their
  father.
- He was their father's favorite son.
- Their father had made him a beautiful coat of many
  colors and had not made coats for his brothers.
- He had shared a dream that placed him above his
  brothers.

So when Joseph was approaching his brothers, their animosity toward him spilled out in a terrible conspiracy:

They saw him from afar, and before he came near
to them they conspired against him to kill him.
They said to one another, "Here comes this dreamer.
Come now, let us kill him and throw him into one
of the pits. Then we will say that a fierce animal has
devoured him, and we will see what will become of
his dreams."
GENESIS 37:18-20

Can't you just picture Joseph's brothers taking a lunch
break from moving a flock of meandering sheep to a new pas-
ture? They may have pictured Joseph back home, lounging
around in his pretty coat, dreaming about more conquests.

Then they looked up and saw Joseph in his colorful coat
heading their way. Grumbling started and quickly turned
to real anger. Tempers flared, and someone ventured to
actually suggest that they kill him. Maybe they had been

commiserating together for years about their favored baby brother. We don't know how long it took them to get to this boiling point, but here they were.

Sometimes as we read the Bible, we're surprised at the things God's chosen people did. To mention just a few in Joseph's ancestry: Rebekah deceived Isaac by plotting against his blessing for Esau; Jacob deceived Isaac by carrying out his mother's plot and received Esau's blessing; Laban, Rebekah's brother, promised his daughter Rachel to Jacob. But he deceived Jacob, and Jacob married Leah, thinking she was Rachel. . . . This is beginning to sound like a modern-day soap opera.

In Joseph's story, we now have the descendants of Jacob plotting to kill their brother. From one generation to another, we see this sin continuing: live by your own standards to get what you want. Even the desire for a blessing became a reason to deceive.

Joseph Forgives His Brothers

Joseph's story is so compelling that it's been presented in several venues, including the popular Broadway musical *Joseph and the Amazing Technicolor Dreamcoat*. I don't know how God's role in that story was portrayed in the Broadway musical, or if it was woven into the story at all. But I do know that God played the major role in the workings of Joseph's life and brought healing to a family caught in the deceit of lies.

Let's look at a brief summary of the adventures that took

Joseph from living a privileged life at home to living as a slave in a country far away.

His scheming brothers wanted to kill him and throw him into one of the pits that dotted the area. Reuben saved Joseph from death, which resulted in his brothers selling him as a slave to a passing caravan of Ishmaelites.

The brothers took his coat from him, slaughtered a goat, dipped the coat in the goat's blood, went home, and showed the coat to their father. He assumed that Joseph had been killed by a fierce animal.

Joseph was taken to Egypt, where God blessed him with favor from Pharaoh's captain of the guard, Potiphar. Potiphar's wife lied about Joseph seducing her, and he landed in prison. And yet Genesis 39:21 says, "But the LORD was with Joseph and showed him steadfast love and gave him favor in the sight of the keeper of the prison."

Joseph used his gift of interpreting dreams while in prison. After Pharaoh heard about this accurate dream seer, he released Joseph from prison and made him the second-most powerful man in Egypt.

Pharaoh's dreams and Joseph's interpretations led to the saving of grain for a coming famine. All the lands around Egypt suffered greatly, but Egypt had grain to spare. When Joseph's brothers traveled to Egypt to buy grain, they found themselves in front of Joseph. He recognized them, but they did not recognize him. After a period of testing his brothers, Joseph brought them before him again.

Joseph was so moved by seeing his brothers and hearing

their story of his father that forgiveness welled up inside of him. Genesis 45:4-5 says, "So Joseph said to his brothers, 'Come near to me, please.' And they came near. And he said, 'I am your brother, Joseph, whom you sold into Egypt. And now do not be distressed or angry with yourselves because you sold me here, for God sent me before you to preserve life.'"

Joseph and his father were reunited, and the whole family moved to Egypt. God restored them and turned the curse of deceit into a blessing.

Yet Joseph didn't seem to forgive his brothers immediately. They had delivered a deep wound to his soul many years earlier when they sold him into slavery. It wasn't Joseph's fault that he was his father's favorite son or that he had the gift of dream interpretation. He could have been a bit wiser about which interpretations to share, but he was young and enthusiastic. His insensitivity was certainly not a reason to consider killing him and, ultimately, to sell him into slavery.

Joseph suffered not only from his brothers' betrayal but also from the lies of Potiphar's wife, which landed him in prison. Joseph had a lot to forgive. But over the years, the Lord's "steadfast love and favor" helped heal Joseph. He may not have been thinking about his brothers at all by the time they arrived before him. Or, he may have worried continually about them and his father as the famine swept the land.

We don't know how the process of forgiveness moved forward in Joseph's life, but seeing his brothers and hearing about his father softened his heart. He embraced them and offered them forgiveness, grace, and love.

Forgiveness doesn't always mean reconciliation, but in this case it did.

Receiving Forgiveness

Because of the goodness of God, Joseph's brothers received forgiveness. They apparently accepted it since they did as Joseph told them to do and enjoyed his blessings of a new and comfortable life.

Sometimes it's hard for us to receive the forgiveness God offers us. Most receivers of generational curses blame themselves for the sinful attitude or behavior of the person who has hurt them, especially if that person is a beloved family member. A father's alcohol abuse or a mother's detachment may render great harm on their children, but we often hear those children voice concern that they did something to cause the painful fallout from their parent's behavior. The remnants of that self-blame can prevent these people, even as adults, from forgiving themselves for something they did not cause in the first place. Many years of incorrect thinking and negative self-talk need to be replaced with the positive reality of how God accepts and loves them.

At other times, these adults look back on poor choices they made as a result of coping with a generational curse and need to receive forgiveness for those choices. I'm a prime example of that scenario. I developed poor self-esteem and believed a lie about my value in life. I coped with those feelings by behaving badly and thinking my value was wrapped up in sinful relationships with men. It sure took me well into adulthood to believe that God could forgive my multiple poor choices. I didn't believe it until that night in my backyard after confessing to Alan that I'd had an affair.

It was total brokenness that allowed me to accept Christ completely and turn my life around. I surrendered everything to Him, including any attempts to cope with the pain of generational sin by looking for love in all the wrong places.

I also needed the help of a counselor to understand and heal from my past. Like God's steadfast love for Joseph, God's steadfast love for me gave me the power to accept His forgiveness. In time, I could also forgive others, including my mother. She had also made poor choices, like encouraging me to have an abortion, because of how she grew up. I hoped she could understand that and receive God's love and forgiveness herself.

A Lifetime of Struggle

My mother and I had a strained relationship for most of her life. Some of that was because of her shame over my behavior and pregnancy, but some of it was due to unresolved issues in her family of origin.

The death of many loved ones hit my mother hard around 2011, when my brother, Ray, passed away from cirrhosis of the liver, emphysema, and COPD. My dad had died in 2004 from metastasized lung cancer, and my sister, Barbara, had died at the age of forty-nine in 2008 from experiencing three grand mal seizures in a row due to mixing drugs and alcohol. My mother's grandson, Logan, died in 2010, and now Ray was dying too. By the time of Ray's illness, my mother's mental capacity and physical health were diminishing. Life was a struggle for her that seemed to overwhelm her ability to forgive or feel forgiven herself.

One day I was at the hospital visiting Ray, and I realized he was very near the end of his earthly life. I said a number of loving things that amounted to a good-bye.

The next morning I woke to a phone message from my mother that Ray had died around 3:00 a.m. I had not heard the phone and told her how sorry I was that I had missed the call. She was furious with me. I told her I had said my good-bye to Ray the day before, but she couldn't receive my apology. I knew she was terribly upset and hoped she would not carry her anger toward me for very long. Unfortunately, her spirit of unforgiveness usually lasted a long time. This time was no different.

During Ray's illness, she had also been very upset with another relative. She complained about this relative a lot and was holding grudges about a number of things. I tried to tell her to let go of those grudges and choose forgiveness. She thought I was taking sides and choosing the other relative over her. I just wanted her to release the hold that bitterness had on her.

When I'd quote some Scripture to her, she'd say, "I don't care what the Bible says. I'll have my revenge." My mom was struggling with her old problem of loving others condition-ally, which she had learned so well.

I faced the reality that my mother and I had nothing in common. Trying to talk to her about forgiveness and the teachings of the Bible had only made her mad. And it didn't help matters when I learned about her erratic driving and wouldn't let one of my grandchildren ride with her.

Unfortunately, my mother saw me as her enemy. Our relationship was strained, and sometimes she was so harsh with me that I struggled to stay in contact with her. I knew I had forgiven her for past hurts, and I was now trying to have a relationship with her as new hurts continued.

As I've said before, forgiveness doesn't necessarily mean reconciliation. That's true. But I had worked hard on for-giving myself and forgiving others, and I felt able to cope with my mother's harshness. I prayed a lot about not being judgmental and understanding how the many recent losses had affected my mother. I talked with a friend who was a counselor and with Al when I felt any spirit of unforgiveness creeping into my thinking.

We were still in this limited relationship when my mother's health began its final decline. Near the end of her life, I talked with her again about how much God loved and forgave her. I encouraged her to have faith replace her fear of being unforgiven. She had accepted Jesus as her Savior, so she could pass from this life of pain into the presence of God in heaven. She passed away at her home on May 12, 2018.

Breaking Generational Curses

Unbroken generational curses allow bitterness to grow in our hearts. At the same time, we are called to forgive others and ourselves when we put our faith in Jesus Christ and endeavor to walk with Him.

The kind of forgiveness that goes out to perpetuators of abuse is, indeed, desperate. It takes supernatural help that results in benefits beyond our imagination.

If you see yourself or your family in the stories in this chapter, *pay attention*! Look at the inner workings of your family relationships. Is there evidence of harmful attitudes or behaviors that you suspect but have not addressed? Determine to investigate and find out the truth of what may lie beneath the surface. In the meantime, whether you see anything wrong or not, do teach your children to know what is appropriate behavior toward them and what is not.

My mother and I were both sexually abused by someone in our families. That doesn't mean that our children would have been sexually abused in the same way, but it did cause Al and me to put safeguards in place for our girls that were not in place for my mother or me. We talked with them when they were old enough to be with other people without us present and told them it was not okay for others to touch them anywhere that the touch made them feel uncomfortable, including their private parts. We told them to tell us immediately if they didn't feel comfortable around someone, if they were afraid of anyone, if they were asked to do something they didn't want to do, or if they were confused about any interaction with anyone—and we meant *anyone*! We didn't want them to be afraid of people, but they needed to know that this caution included family and friends. We also made a point of telling them that there wasn't anything they could do that would make us unhappy with them.

Protecting your children and grandchildren is an ongoing process of educating them while reinforcing your love and acceptance of them.

There are a lot of different generational curses out there, but the steps to breaking them are amazingly similar:

1. Decide that you are not going to be bound any longer by the weight of a particular curse.
2. Ask God to deliver you from the curse.
3. Declare your decision to break a generational curse to God and to other people.
4. Fight daily to never return to living a cursed life.
5. Share your victories with other people.
6. Remember daily that Satan blinds people to the generational curses they live with.
7. Rebuke Satan!
8. Turn back to the Lord and ask for His protection from the enemy.

Write down these steps and refer to them often.

It's hard to break old habits of thoughts and actions. You need to keep reinforcing your decision to break whatever generational curse has been passed on to you. Going through this process will begin to free you from bitterness toward others who have passed on sinful attitudes and behaviors to you or others in your family. You will receive the blessings of God and the blessings of living as forgivers and the forgiven.

So: decide, ask, declare, fight, share, remember, rebuke, turn back, and write!

It was difficult for me to learn to really forgive my mother for her conditional love for me and stay in relationship with her. And even though I had little contact with my abuser, it was very hard to forgive him in my heart.

But God's love toward me and His mercy in forgiving me for all my sins transformed my heart and released me to forgive others.

Every time Al and I share our story of healing and breaking the bonds of generational curses, we thicken the scar tissue over our old wounds. Helping others break free strengthens us in our own battles with Satan, the accuser of the saints. A new and peaceful life is possible when we allow God to break our chains of bondage.

CHAPTER 11

FORGIVING
THE PRODIGALS

AFTER MY (AL'S) BABY BROTHER, Jep, started college, he embraced Halloween as an opportunity to consume larger than usual quantities of alcohol and drugs with his rowdy college friends. One year, he succeeded so well at this mission that we could see and smell the results the next morning.

As the darkness of the evening gradually gave way to bright morning sunlight, a stunning scene was revealed. There, on one side of a remote Louisiana gravel road, was a big green Chevy pickup truck. The driver's side door was open, but the driver's seat where Jep had been sitting was empty. He was on the ground, with only his right leg stretched up and resting uncomfortably on the floor of the truck.

The rest of Jep was sprawled out on the gravel road. He was unconscious and covered with big, bloody scratches.

As soon as he woke up, he would realize his body was freezing cold and his head was being split in two by one of the worst hangovers of his young life. But it would be a while before he came to. Meanwhile, flies and ants went in and out of his open mouth, and each breath he exhaled smelled like something really bad had died deep down inside him.

Nobody knew how long Jep had been lying there in the road, or how he had wound up in this perilous situation, or how many other vehicles or people he had encountered along the way. All we knew was that things had been going downhill for Jep for quite some time, even though he had done his best to cover up his sins by living a double life. He was one person with his rowdy friends, but he tried to act like he was a completely different person when he was around family members, the Duck Commander offices, or our church.

Few of us had any notion that he was spiraling out of control until that morning after Halloween, even though we could detect signs that all was not well with our brother. But now the mess that was his life was right out there in the open for anyone to see. The family started plotting and scheming his recovery, and soon we would all get together to confront him with the sad facts of his sorry life.

But first, I had some of my own spiritual housekeeping to take care of. Even though I had gone through my own periods of rowdiness and reckless behavior, I felt myself sitting in judgment over my baby brother and his sins. I wrestled with whether or not to extend him the forgiveness that had been so life-changing to me and so essential to my recovery.

I was the pastor of the church our family attended, and most pastors don't take kindly to hypocrites who go wild all week but try to pretend they're faithful followers of Christ for a couple of hours on Sunday morning. Jep had continued to attend Sunday services during his period of sowing his wild oats, but I found myself getting angry at my brother, who nodded along with my sermons but ignored all the biblical teaching and life lessons I presented. And even though Lisa and I had experienced our own versions of desperate forgiveness in our lives, I wasn't so sure Jep deserved that kind of forgiveness in his current state.

It wasn't that my theology had changed. I still believed in Christ's forgiveness for our sins. But long-buried family issues and resentments were rising to the surface, and these conflicted feelings were complicating my response. My baby brother needed my love and grace, but for some reason I didn't fully understand, I was unable to extend these blessings to him.

I felt slightly uneasy about my judgmental attitude toward Jep, and soon God would find an interesting way to make me feel uneasy enough to do something about it.

Inside the Pastor's Study

I love working on sermons. My process starts with studying passages of Scripture and researching those passages in Bible commentaries and studies. After I feel that I understand the key message the passages convey, I begin organizing my thoughts and thinking of the various stories and anecdotes I can use to drive the message home.

But as I prepared to give a series of sermons on the ministry of Christ as found in the Gospel of Luke, I ran into a brick wall when I got to Luke 15. It's a chapter of the New Testament that contains three powerful parables, each of which was increasing my uneasy feelings about what was going on with Jep.

First up was Christ's parable of the lost sheep:

Now the tax collectors and sinners were all drawing near to hear him. And the Pharisees and the scribes grumbled, saying, "This man receives sinners and eats with them."

So he told them this parable: "What man of you, having a hundred sheep, if he has lost one of them, does not leave the ninety-nine in the open country, and go after the one that is lost, until he finds it? And when he has found it, he lays it on his shoulders, rejoicing. And when he comes home, he calls together his friends and his neighbors, saying to them, 'Rejoice with me, for I have found my sheep that was lost.' Just so, I tell you, there will be more joy in heaven over one sinner who repents than over ninety-nine righteous persons who need no repentance."

LUKE 15:1-7

I have always loved this parable about the man who leaves behind the ninety-nine sheep who are doing what they are supposed to be doing to rescue the one sheep who was lost. In fact, there have been times when I felt that was what God had done for me: temporarily neglected ninety-nine righteous folks to save and redeem a sinner like me.

This is one of many New Testament passages featuring the Pharisees, who were a Jewish religious group at the time of Jesus. In the New Testament, the Pharisees are portrayed as preferring God's law over God's grace. These legal-minded men tangled with Jesus, just as they had tangled with John the Baptist.

For example, when Gentiles (people who were not Jewish) became Christians after Christ's death, the Pharisees insisted that these Christian converts must be circumcised and follow all the Mosaic laws that Jews followed. Meanwhile, Paul and other early Christian evangelists insisted that men and women who accepted Christ did not need to live in accordance with the many behavioral dictates of Jewish law.

I had always enjoyed seeing Jesus battle the legalistic Pharisees He came into contact with throughout His ministry, but suddenly, as I reread this famous passage, I could feel part of me rebelling against this parable of grace and love for the lost. I was particularly stuck on this whole idea of leaving the ninety-nine for the one.

What if I applied similar numerical reasoning to duck hunting? *There is no way this math would work during our family duck-hunting adventures*, I thought. *I know what would happen if we had successfully shot ninety-nine ducks, but I decided to leave these ninety-nine ducks behind and go out in search of one additional duck. I'm sure everyone would let me know how crazy an idea that is.*

And what if I applied similar numerical reasoning to church? *What a silly thing it would be for a pastor who had a church of ninety-nine righteous people to forget about them and instead go in search of the one person who was unrighteous and needed salvation,* I told myself. *And what would happen if some of those ninety-nine believers suddenly quit attending this church, taking their weekly offering with them?*

But I was brought back to my senses by the parable's conclusion, which emphasized the joy Christ experiences each time a sinner repents and accepts Him into their lives.

Facing My Anger

Christ's next parable in Luke 15 makes the same point with a different set of props. Instead of sheep, Jesus shifts the focus to a lost coin:

> Or what woman, having ten silver coins, if she loses one coin, does not light a lamp and sweep the house and seek diligently until she finds it? And when she has found it, she calls together her friends and neighbors, saying, "Rejoice with me, for I have found the coin that I had lost." Just so, I tell you, there is joy before the angels of God over one sinner who repents.
>
> LUKE 15:8-10

I know some people today have a difficult time understanding the woman in this parable or comprehending why she was so desperate for that one coin. But I have no problem understanding this story. Having grown up in poverty myself, I can see why a woman would diligently search her entire house for one missing coin. The story actually reminds me of growing up with my two younger brothers Willie and Jase as Miss Kay did all she could to provide for us while our father was AWOL.

But this parable isn't about poor country people trying to scrape together enough coins to survive for another day. It's about the joy experienced in heaven when one sinner repents and accepts Christ's gift of forgiveness.

Still, somehow I couldn't let go of the poverty angle, and the more I thought about it, the more I realized what my problem was. I was angry at Jep because I felt he got a much better deal as the fourth child in the family than Willie, Jase, and I had experienced when we were growing up.

When the Past Lives On

I was born into a mess. As I indicated in chapters 1 and 2, Miss Kay was never planning on becoming a pregnant teenager, particularly with a ne'er-do-well boyfriend like Phil Robertson, who at the time would rather be off fishing and drinking than being a dad. By the time I was eight years old, the five of us—Mom, Dad, and the three oldest kids—were crammed together in a one-room trailer near that run-down bar that Phil managed.

It was a short time later that Phil—who was often angry and occasionally abusive—told my mom and the three of us kids to get out of his life. That separation was painful for me, since I didn't know if I would ever see my father again. The one father figure in my life was gone.

As everyone knows, Phil finally got over his "rompin' stompin'" days, returned to the family, accepted Christ as his Savior, repented of his sins, and began anew. I was unbelievably grateful to see Dad back, particularly since he was living a new life.

But the pains and sorrows I had endured as a youngster weren't erased from my memory banks because of Phil's sudden, dramatic conversion. There's a big area in a boy's heart that grows cold and lonely when it's not warmed by a father's love, and I had spent more time than I cared to without that fatherly affection.

As I prepared my sermon series, I could see how the experiences I had gone through were messing up my relationship with my baby brother. Jep knew that his three older brothers had gone through horrendous times before Dad became a Christian. But by the time Jep arrived on the scene, the Robertsons looked pretty much like a normal family, complete with a mom and dad who loved each other. The whole family went to church together on Sundays, and during the week we all worked at Duck Commander, the company that Phil had started once he got his life straightened out.

It seemed to me that Jep never really appreciated all the good things he enjoyed: a happy family that was spiritually and financially stable, with a decent place to live and plenty of food for everyone to eat. During our family's tough years, I would have given anything to enjoy these benefits, but to Jep they seemed to be no big deal, and that was getting under my skin and making it harder for me to forgive Jep's wayward ways.

Soon enough, God would have an opportunity to confront my lack of forgiveness.

When Good Boys Go Bad

Jep was the fourth and final son of Phil and Kay Robertson, and like the rest of us, he had the freedom to embrace or reject the devotion to Christ he saw all around him in his family. Eventually he found a faith in Christ that was his own. It happened naturally, as Jep saw Christ transform other people's lives in dramatic ways.

Every Sunday night Phil and Kay had a house church meeting in their home with about eight other couples. Phil also attracted many sinners and seekers who asked him all the questions they had about God. After these conversations, Phil often wound up baptizing new converts in the river near our house.

Looking on, Jep could see the reality of spiritual transformation. People who came to the house looking as if they were carrying unimaginable burdens of sorrow and sin would, over time, lighten up as they experienced the joy of salvation. Jep had been around enough to know the difference between people who were truly transformed and those who were merely pretending. Jep knew God was real because he could see God working in other people's lives. When Jep was thirteen years old, he finally felt ready to be baptized by Phil in the river too.

All went well, at least until it didn't. Jep had worked hard on his basketball moves, and by high school he was a star on the local team. But then the first in a series of disasters struck. Jep broke his ankle in a scrimmage game the summer before his junior year. With that one mistaken move, Jep's high-school basketball career ended and his identity as a sports star was lost. Now he felt like a big nobody.

Jep then poured all his energy into girls, but when a girl-friend he really liked broke up with him, that part of his life and identity was suddenly gone too. After that, Jep pretty much sought pleasure wherever he could find it, filling his life with alcohol, drugs, and sexual relationships.

We could tell things weren't right, but because Jep was so successful at living a secret life, we didn't know how bad things had gotten. As he writes in his own book, "I became a master at hiding my secret life and pretending everything was fine."[1]

He officially held a job at Duck Commander and received regular paychecks, but his work attendance was spotty at best. He faithfully attended church, but I could tell he was there for girls, not God. One day he and one of our cousins came to church with their hair bleached a brilliant white. Everybody whispered about it in the pews. Jep loved that.

One thing led to another, and before long, Jep lay on a gravel road on the morning after Halloween, with one leg on the roadway and the other still up in his truck. As the sun rose higher in the sky, Jep eventually woke up, spat the ants out of his mouth, unsteadily rose to his feet, dusted himself off, and drove back to the apartment he shared with his college buddies. By evening time, he would be drinking and drugging again.

Meanwhile, the other members of the Robertson family had hatched a plan.

The Intervention

The Monday after Halloween, Willie was teaching a small Bible study for students at the nearby University of Louisiana Monroe. Jep showed up that night, perhaps because he was feeling guilty about some of his latest antics.

"I know some of you are struggling hard," Willie told the group. Jep didn't realize Willie was talking straight to him.

A couple nights later Jep went to the movies. He was drunk as a skunk once again. His buddy gave him a ride home, and Jep left his truck at the theater. When he came back the next morning to pick up his truck, there was a note stuck under the windshield wiper.

"I know what you've been up to," said the note, written by Willie. "We need to talk. I'll meet you at Dad's."

When Jep drove up to the family homestead later that morning, he was confronted by an armada of trucks. We were all there waiting for him. Jep entered the main room, his hair still bleached white, and his earlobes sporting earrings. Phil was the first to speak to him.

"Put the keys to *my* truck in *my* hand."

Phil was referring to the truck that I've been calling "Jep's truck" throughout this chapter. But it wasn't really Jep's truck. Dad owned it. Jep silently handed Dad the keys.

Phil had a follow-up question ready to go. "Well, Son, are you ready to change your life?"

That sobered up Jep real quick.

Phil continued with his offer. "All of us have come to a decision as a family. We are offering you two choices. Choice one is you can keep doing what you're doing. We don't know if you will live through that or not, but if that's your choice we don't want anything to do with you. One of us can drop you off at the highway, and you will be on your own to live your life as you want.

"I think you know what choice two is. You can join this family again, follow God as we do, and live your life on the values we stand for. And if you make this choice, you will be living with us here, and you will be forbidden from seeing your old friends. There will be no more drinking or doing drugs with them. You have to give all that up.

"Those are your two choices."

Some of us thought Jep would put up some resistance, but he quickly gave his answer.

"What took you all so long?" he asked us. "I know I don't deserve to come back home, but I want to come back. Will you take me back?"

"My prodigal son has returned home," Phil said, tears streaming down his cheeks. Phil wasn't much of a crier. I had only seen him cry two times before. But when we saw him breaking down, all the rest of us started crying too.

But none of us were sobbing as loud as Jep, who was writhing on the floor. All of us gathered around him, laid our hands on him, and prayed for him until he calmed down.

It was a wonderful reunion, and for the foreseeable future, Jep would be under the Robertson version of house arrest. As far as his drinking and drugging friends were concerned, Jep was about to go missing in action.

Meanwhile, I returned to my sermon preparation, where once again I was confronted by my own judgmental attitude toward my baby brother.

God's Sermon to Me

I knew it would happen sooner or later. My sermons on the Gospel of Luke had now brought me to Jesus' parable of the Prodigal Son. But as I studied this powerful passage, trying to see how I could preach it to my church, I could hear Christ preaching *to me* about my own self-righteous anger toward Jep.

My uneasy feelings grew stronger as I studied the three parts of the Prodigal Son parable.

1. Jesus starts the parable by describing the sinful son:

There was a man who had two sons. And the younger of them said to his father, "Father, give me

the share of property that is coming to me." And
he divided his property between them. Not many
days later, the younger son gathered all he had and
took a journey into a far country, and there he
squandered his property in reckless living. And when
he had spent everything, a severe famine arose in
that country, and he began to be in need. So he went
and hired himself out to one of the citizens of that
country, who sent him into his fields to feed pigs.
And he was longing to be fed with the pods that the
pigs ate, and no one gave him anything.

But when he came to himself, he said, "How many
of my father's hired servants have more than enough
bread, but I perish here with hunger! I will arise and
go to my father, and I will say to him, 'Father, I have
sinned against heaven and before you. I am no longer
worthy to be called your son. Treat me as one of your
hired servants.'" And he arose and came to his father.

LUKE 15:11-20

So far, the parable seemed like a perfect fit for Jep's wayward life. Jep had been living nearby, so it would be difficult
to say he had traveled to a "far country," but his wild period
had certainly taken him far away from the Christian values
he grew up with all of his life.

When Jep returned to us for the family intervention,
his attitude of regret and repentance reminded me of the
younger brother in Jesus' parable.

2. The brief middle part of the parable deals with the father's response to the return of his prodigal son:

> But while he was still a long way off, his father saw
> him and felt compassion, and ran and embraced him
> and kissed him. And the son said to him, "Father,
> I have sinned against heaven and before you. I am no
> longer worthy to be called your son." But the father
> said to his servants, "Bring quickly the best robe,
> and put it on him, and put a ring on his hand, and
> shoes on his feet. And bring the fattened calf and kill
> it, and let us eat and celebrate. For this my son was
> dead, and is alive again; he was lost, and is found."
> And they began to celebrate.
>
> LUKE 15:20-24

Jesus was a master storyteller, and when we hear this brief passage, we can feel the father's emotions. This father thought his son was dead, or at least nearly so. Now he was back and fully alive. Who wouldn't want to celebrate?

The answer to that question is found in the final portion of the parable, which describes the less than enthusiastic response of the older brother.

3. The final part of the parable deals with the older brother's judgmental response to the prodigal's return:

> Now his older son was in the field, and as he came
> and drew near to the house, he heard music and

dancing. And he called one of the servants and asked what these things meant. And he said to him, "Your brother has come, and your father has killed the fattened calf, because he has received him back safe and sound." But he was angry and refused to go in. His father came out and entreated him, but he answered his father, "Look, these many years I have served you, and I never disobeyed your command, yet you never gave me a young goat, that I might celebrate with my friends. But when this son of yours came, who has devoured your property with prostitutes, you killed the fattened calf for him!" And he said to him, "Son, you are always with me, and all that is mine is yours. It was fitting to celebrate and be glad, for this your brother was dead, and is alive; he was lost, and is found."

LUKE 15:25-32

Many of the details in this final portion of the parable are dramatically different from details of Jep's return to the fold. In our case, there was no music, dancing, or servants. And instead of the fatted calf, we dined on fatted catfish.

But once you dig beneath the details and look at what is going on in people's hearts, the story of the prodigal fit my situation perfectly. Yes, I actually was angry at Jep. And if there had been music and dancing, I would have been in no mood to join the happy throng.

I looked again at the parables of the lost sheep, the lost coin, and the Prodigal Son, and I considered my life. The conclusion I drew was disturbing. When it came to my baby brother, I was a self-righteous Pharisee. In my youth, I had been more than glad to be a prodigal son who left for a time of wildness and debauchery. Then I'd come to my senses, repented, and returned home to the loving embrace of my family.

But now that Jep was the wayward prodigal, I was playing the role of the legalist who was judging his heart and pronouncing him unworthy of God's forgiveness. The parallels between me and the Pharisees were everywhere to see:

- I was angry. *(I'm not going to celebrate someone else's forgiveness and redemption!)*

- I was haughty. *(I have cleaned up my own act and been obedient to Christ for three years, but Jep hasn't done any of this important spiritual work!)*

- I was jealous. *(The family was enjoying a big meal to welcome Jep back, but I don't remember a big celebration for me when I returned from my wayward ways!)*

- I was accusatory. *(You know, Jep's sins are probably more numerous than mine were. Are we really sure we want to forgive all this wrongdoing he has been responsible for?)*

It's curious to me that the final portion of the parable ends with the father encouraging the older brother to lay down his negative feelings and join the celebration for the returned prodigal. The parable doesn't tell us if the older brother accepted this advice from his father.

That's the beauty of Christ's parables. Not only do they tell interesting stories, but they challenge us to see how we will respond. The parable of the Prodigal Son nailed my attitude exactly, and it wasn't pretty.

Before long, I came to my senses. I asked God to forgive me for my judgmental attitude and experienced Christ forgiving me for my own lack of forgiveness. Then I asked Jep to forgive me too. He did. Suddenly the distance that had grown between us seemed to disappear.

Over the years, Jep and I have had a few opportunities to give our twinned testimonies standing together on a stage. It has been a phenomenal blessing for us to be able to share our stories. Our audiences seem to connect with the journeys we two desperate prodigals have taken since experiencing the all-surpassing forgiveness of God.

When You Feel like the Older Brother

My experiences with Jep confirmed a number of powerful lessons, and these lessons aren't restricted to actual blood brothers.

Lesson number one seems pretty clear: don't get bent out of shape about people God chooses to forgive. It seems that it's surprisingly easy for people who have received Christ's gift of forgiveness to turn around and deny that gift to others who need it, either through our attitudes or our actions.

When we (Al and Lisa) were desperate for God's forgiveness, we felt joy and relief and gratitude when that love and mercy were graciously granted to us. But when we thought about the ugly sins of *other people*, we were somehow much less excited about Christ's extravagance.

It doesn't matter whether you're upset about your prodigal baby brother or a stranger who shows up at your church smelling of alcohol or marijuana. We are the body of Christ, and our job is to extend Christ's love to everyone. God has accepted some sinful scoundrels into His family; now we need to accept them into our family of faith.

Here's another lesson: forgiveness isn't a one-time event but an ongoing process that continues throughout our lives. Even though Christ has long ago forgiven us for some of our biggest and baddest sins, we need to remain desperate for His forgiveness day after day, moment by moment, as we commit new sins, whether big or small.

It's a fact of life: people sin and do all kinds of horrible, stupid, and self-destructive things. What kind of attitude do we want to have when these people repent and cry out to God for forgiveness? Do we want to rejoice with the angels in heaven, or do we want to stand outside with the Pharisees and the grumpy older brother, steaming about the ways God lavishes His love on other people?

Each of us has to make this choice: rejoice or grumble. We thank God He has shown us how to rejoice.

You may not have a younger brother, but who is it you don't want to forgive?

CHAPTER 12

LIVING A LIFE OF FORGIVENESS

Jesus had been teaching the crowds, healing people's ailments, and telling His disciples more details about His upcoming death and resurrection. Everything seemed sober and serious as Jesus taught about marriage and divorce, sin and salvation, life and death.

That's when the disturbance happened. People started bringing children and infants to see Jesus and be touched by Him. Children tend to interrupt adults' serious talks, and they certainly did so this day, offending Jesus' disciples. The disciples decided to take matters into their own hands, act rapidly, and calm things down. Luke says they "rebuked" the people for bringing their children. (See Luke 18:15.)

Someone didn't appreciate the harsh tone the disciples used to criticize the people, and He spoke up, as Mark's Gospel tells us: "But when Jesus saw it, he was indignant" (Mark 10:14).

Can you picture Jesus' negative reaction toward His disciples? Mark doesn't tell us any more details about Jesus' emotions. We don't know whether He was angry or merely annoyed with His disciples for their latest shenanigans. But His words conveyed a powerful message: "'Let the children come to me; do not hinder them, for to such belongs the kingdom of God. Truly, I say to you, whoever does not receive the kingdom of God like a child shall not enter it.' And he took them in his arms and blessed them, laying his hands on them" (Mark 10:14-16).

As we close this book, we want to piggyback on these words of Jesus. Our mission is to bring sinners into the presence of Christ, where they can experience forgiveness and salvation.

Let the sinners come to Him, we plead. Do not hinder them from drawing close, because Christ came to bring forgiveness to sinners. Jesus didn't like it when His disciples served as barriers, preventing people from being near Him and experiencing His love. Think for a moment about some of the people Jesus forgave: people who had little or no faith; women caught in sexual sin; tax collectors who oppressed the Jewish people; and even a criminal who had been crucified and was hanging on a cross the same day Jesus was crucified.

Even as He was near death, Jesus was consumed with forgiving His enemies and those who had sentenced Him to death. Looking down from the cross, He could see soldiers gambling to determine who would win His clothing. He could see crowds jeering at Him and cheering His crucifixion. He could see the religious leaders who had worked for so long to trap Him in doctrinal disputes. Now they were mocking Him.

As He looked down at all these people, He uttered a simple but profound prayer: "Father, forgive them, for they know not what they do" (Luke 23:34).

If you are a sinner, don't let your guilt, shame, grief, and anger keep you from the mercy of God. If Christ can forgive the men who mocked and crucified Him, He can forgive you if you repent of your sins.

Redeemed by Grace

Sin is dark and destructive, and as it ripples through relationships and families, it can pollute and destroy those relationships. Thank God that our marriage and our families have experienced the freedom forgiveness can bring.

Forgiveness made the Robertson family healthy and whole again.

Forgiveness empowered Lisa to overcome generational sin within her family.

Forgiveness allowed us (Lisa and Al) to be reconciled and to reboot our marriage.

Forgiveness enabled the two of us to overcome our

challenges and learn to love each other more deeply day by day. Now forgiveness flows through our marriage to our children, and to their children, and to anyone else we come in contact with.

There will always be those who feel they need to erect barriers to keep people from flocking to Jesus. But don't let these people stop you from bringing your brokenness and sin to the One who has the divine authority to forgive our sins. And once you have experienced even a taste of that forgiveness, don't ever let yourself be a barrier that would prevent anyone else from experiencing this relief.

The Road to Redemption: Thirteen Disciplines for Living a Life of Forgiveness

Many of the questions people ask when we're speaking about forgiveness fall into the category we call the "Now what?" questions. People ask these "Now what?" questions when they are trying to figure out how to walk in Christ's forgiving footsteps.

You may have some "Now what?" questions of your own after reading this book. So before you file this book on your bookshelf with others you have read, and promptly forget much of what we talked about, let us use our remaining pages to give you the tools you need to make forgiveness a daily reality in your life and relationships.

Since we view the life of forgiveness as a journey, we are giving you disciplines you can use to help you on this journey. Ready to start?

Discipline 1: Seek forgiveness now!

We have shared sad, even depressing stories of desperate forgiveness in this book. Most of the people in these stories were broken, lonely men and women whose daily lives were shot through with sorrow, loss, pain, and regret. In most—but not all—of the stories, people's desperation eventually led them to seek forgiveness.

But things could have turned out much better if everyone had learned to practice our first discipline: seek forgiveness now! The many scenarios we've described would have turned out far better far sooner, and fewer people would have been hurt, if everyone had sought forgiveness when they first encountered problems rather than waiting and waiting as their problems mounted.

We've told you stories of desperate forgiveness we have seen firsthand, but we have an important announcement for you: you don't need to wait until you become equally desperate before seeking forgiveness from God or from the people you have hurt. Instead of continuing to abuse yourself and the people who are trying to love you, confess your sins and sorrows to Jesus and receive His forgiveness.

Some people seem to treat forgiveness like laundry. Instead of keeping up with their dirty laundry by doing a load or two when clothes start piling up, they prefer to let their entire laundry room fill up with dirty clothes before attacking the huge pile. That approach may work for laundry, but we run into problems when we apply that same approach to seeking forgiveness. When we don't regularly deal with the "dirty laundry" in our lives, our unconfessed sin soon piles up, taking up more and more space in our hearts and minds.

When is the last time you prayed and confessed your sins to God? If it has been a while, take the advice of Isaiah and set a time for confession now:

> Seek the LORD while he may be found;
>   call upon him while he is near.
>
> ISAIAH 55:6

Discipline 2: Continually seek forgiveness as a way of life

Both of us make forgiveness a regular part of our daily lives. We're convinced that forgiveness shouldn't be reserved for special occasions or for "big sins" like murder or adultery. Forgiveness should instead be a regular part of daily life, because it's just as important as eating and sleeping. Practicing forgiveness on a daily basis leads to something we call living a life of forgiveness.

We compare the life of forgiveness to getting regular oil changes for your car. If you don't get regular oil changes, your oil will get dirty and your car won't work as well. But if you get regular oil changes, your engine will run more smoothly and last longer.

It's similar with forgiveness. Both of us seek forgiveness every day because we've seen how this "daily maintenance routine" helps keep our lives and our relationships running smoothly.

Al's daily forgiveness routine goes like this: "In the

morning after I wake up, I thank God for His new mercies for the new day. My prayers typically go something like this: 'God, I know yesterday is gone, and my mistakes and sins are gone with it, thanks to Your mercy and grace. Please help me share and extend that same mercy and grace with everyone I meet today.'"

Al also meditates on this biblical passage:

> The steadfast love of the LORD never ceases;
>   his mercies never come to an end;
> they are new every morning;
>   great is your faithfulness.
>
> LAMENTATIONS 3:22-23

We seek forgiveness daily, hourly, and moment by moment—not because we are more sinful or more saintly than other people, but because we realize we need regular doses of this powerful, healing medicine.

Discipline 3: Forgive them now

Are there people who have hurt and abused you? Does the pain of these offenses burn in your heart, agitate your stomach, or bring tears of grief to your eyes? If you feel you have been sinned against, there's something you will need to do: Let it go. Forgive your offender.

Some of you may be wondering: why do we think it's so important that all of us forgive others who have sinned against us? There are two main reasons.

First, Jesus commands us to forgive. Each of us needs to forgive if we are going to experience forgiveness ourselves. It says so right there in the middle of the Lord's Prayer:

> And he said to them, "When you pray, say:
> 'Father,
> hallowed be your name.
> Your kingdom come.
> Give us each day our daily bread,
> and forgive us our sins,
>   for we ourselves forgive everyone who is indebted
>   to us.
> And lead us not into temptation.'"
>
> LUKE 11:2-4

Second, we need to forgive others so our own minds and hearts don't become overwhelmed with animosity and anger. Some people embrace the idea that they can punish their enemies by holding on to grudges and anger, but holding on to bad feelings doesn't punish our enemies as much as it ruins our own lives.

The writer of the book of Hebrews warned us about this: "Look after each other so that not one of you will fail to find God's best blessings. Watch out that no bitterness takes root among you, for as it springs up it causes deep trouble, hurting many in their spiritual lives" (Hebrews 12:15, TLB). Unresolved bitterness defiles the unforgiver, first and foremost. Then it spreads outward, defiling everyone else it comes in contact with.

We see many people at our seminars weighed down by years and years of unforgiveness. Only when they learn to let it go and forgive those who have hurt them does that weight begin to fall away.

Remember, forgiveness isn't a one-way transaction:

God forgive me.

It's a two-way street:

God forgive me, and God help me forgive.

Is there someone you need to forgive? Search your heart and see who comes to mind. Then get to work on the often difficult work of forgiving their wrongdoing.

Discipline 4: Forgive them again, and again, and again

Perhaps you could see this coming, but when we talk about living a lifestyle of forgiveness, that means continually receiving and giving forgiveness.

The crazed drivers who cut you off on the highway nearly every morning when you're driving to work? Forgive them again and again.

The people at work who regularly talk about you behind your back, or steal your snacks out of the company fridge, or fail to carry their weight around the office? Forgive them again and again.

The relatives and loved ones who seem determined to find new and distressing ways to offend and take advantage of you? Forgive them again and again.

The apostle Peter was a curious disciple who often asked Jesus interesting questions. One day he asked Jesus for advice about how to handle someone who frequently sinned against him: "Then Peter came up and said to Him, 'Lord, how often shall my brother sin against me and I forgive him? Up to seven times?' Jesus said to him, 'I do not say to you, up to seven times, but up to seventy times seven'" (Matthew 18:21-22, NASB).

Does this mean the Bible says we are required to forgive people up to 490 times, but that's the limit? No. Jesus was using numbers to make a point. There's no limit. We must forgive people who sin against us 491 times, or 492 times, or however many more times they seek forgiveness. That's what God does with us.

However, we need to emphasize one important distinction: *forgiving is not the same thing as reconciling.*

Lisa has forgiven the man who abused her when she was a child, but she is not reconciled with him. He has not acknowledged the abuse or apologized for it. Al has forgiven the man who abused Lisa but has no relationship with him. Sin has broken that relationship.

Forgiving and reconciling are related, but they are different processes. Forgiving changes *you*, but it may not change the person you forgive.

Both of us have known opioid addicts who left behind a trail of hurt and mayhem before dying of overdoses. These people are gone now, so there's no way anyone can be reconciled with them. All we can do is forgive them.

Discipline 5: Forgive yourself

We've come to know many people who have been able to forgive others but can't find it in their hearts to forgive themselves. Many of these hurting souls pour their hearts out to Lisa after she shares her experience of having an abortion.

For decades, Christians have worked to reduce the number of abortions, but in taking on this deadly sin, is it possible that some of us have alienated or scared away women who are desperate for Christ's forgiveness? Have we sent the message that this particular sin is too dark and deadly to be washed clean by Christ's love?

We have also counseled people involved in homosexual sin. They may face even greater hostility in some corners. In our zeal to promote the message that marriage is for men and women, not same-sex couples, have we also communicated to gays and lesbians that their sins are somehow worse than everyone else's, or somehow beyond Christ's love and forgiveness?

God hates sin, but He loves sinners. Too often we focus on the first half of that sentence. Let's work on a more balanced and loving approach that invites people to confess their sins to God and receive His forgiveness.

As we saw with the story of the rich young golden boy in chapter 8, not everyone receives forgiveness. The problem isn't with God but with us, as the disciples learned: "And they were exceedingly astonished, and said to him, 'Then who can be saved?' Jesus looked at them and said, 'With man it is impossible, but not with God. For all things are possible with God'" (Mark 10:26-27).

We have seen that forgiving yourself is only possible if you truly believe that God can forgive you—and has. When people are skeptical or doubtful about God forgiving them, believing in forgiveness takes faith: "Without faith it is impossible to please [God], for whoever would draw near to God must believe that he exists and that he rewards those who seek him" (Hebrews 11:6).

Discipline 6: Forget it

Remember Bobby, the man from chapter 8 who spent fifteen years carrying around his guilt about not going to church during the year he was serving in the Army in Germany? Bobby was finally able to bring this sin to God and seek forgiveness.

God can forgive, but can we forget? People like Bobby, who spend years clinging to their guilt over sin, may have more trouble than most in forgetting about their forgiven sins and moving on. When a person obsesses over guilt, it can be hard to get over that obsession.

Memories can be troublesome things. At times, it seems our brains continually remind us of all the bad things we have done, the hurtful ways we have related to other people, the selfishness we indulge.

But God has a different kind of memory. He is somehow able to wipe any trace of forgiven sins from His divine memory bank. Here's how God expressed that thought through the prophet Jeremiah: "I will forgive their iniquity, and I will remember their sin no more" (Jeremiah 31:34— this Old Testament prophecy is also paraphrased in the New Testament, in Hebrews 8:12 and 10:17).

If God can forget your sins, don't you think you should try to do so too? We know there are those people who say, "There is no way that I can ever forget a hurt or sin." But forgiveness brings healing, and with it, the ability to forget past pains.

Discipline 7: Remember your victories over sin, and celebrate them!
In speaking to groups about forgiveness, the two of us repeatedly tell stories about our own past sins. In these cases, we're not trying to forget these destructive episodes; we're trying to recall them in detail so we can share them with people who struggle with forgiveness.

We're not sad when we openly share these stories of sin and redemption. We are joyful and grateful. Sure, there are times when it's not fun to recall some of the darkest moments of our lives, but we also get to remember how God broke through our darkness. We get to celebrate the reality of these victories together each time.

Has forgiveness helped lift the weight of guilt from your shoulders in at least some arenas of your life? Then celebrate that freedom! Don't be stingy with God's wonderful victories!

Discipline 8: Realize you're fighting a lifelong struggle with sin
Sin is like dandelions. Or perhaps sin is like hair that pops up on your body in places where you don't want it. Either

way, it seems that once you try to get rid of sin in one place, it pops up somewhere else.

Increasingly, both men and women seem to be struggling with Internet and video porn. These modern, high-tech tools feed a timeless temptation: lust. Jesus explained the problem in His Sermon on the Mount: "You have heard that it was said, 'You shall not commit adultery.' But I say to you that everyone who looks at a woman with lustful intent has already committed adultery with her in his heart" (Matthew 5:27-28). Our culture makes porn easily accessible to those who want it. But sexually provocative imagery is everywhere. Erotic poses are used to sell products like beer and burgers, or services such as web hosting. The result is a sex-saturated culture that provides a breeding ground for lust.

Men and women struggle with lust and sexual temptation, but we thank God that we can grow into purity and holiness as we carry on a lifelong fight against sin.

Are you struggling right now? Be strong in the fight.

Do you sometimes fall? Don't beat yourself up too badly, but instead, place your heart in Christ's healing hands and seek His cleansing once again.

Commit yourself to continuing the struggle, growing stronger and stronger each day as Christ becomes Lord of more and more parts of your life. Then you will begin to know what it means to overcome sin. And don't hesitate to find Christian counseling if you are having trouble with porn.

When Paul describes life as a race in 1 Corinthians 9:24, he means a marathon, not a brief sprint. When you fall down, get up and keep running. Don't give up or give in. Don't let sin rule you.

Discipline 9: Have you been forgiven much? Then love much
One of the best ways to tell if someone has been deeply forgiven is to see how they treat other people. This isn't coming from Al and Lisa, but from a much higher authority.

Luke's Gospel shares the lovely story of the sinful woman who washed Jesus' feet with her tears, dried them with her hair, kissed them, and then rubbed them with expensive perfume. A Pharisee questioned why Christ would allow a sinful woman to do all of this.

Jesus startled the Pharisee with His response:

> Then turning toward the woman [Jesus] said to Simon, "Do you see this woman? I entered your house; you gave me no water for my feet, but she has wet my feet with her tears and wiped them with her hair. You gave me no kiss, but from the time I came in she has not ceased to kiss my feet. You did not anoint my head with oil, but she has anointed my feet with ointment. Therefore I tell you, her sins, which are many, are forgiven—for she loved much. But he who is forgiven little, loves little."
>
> LUKE 7:44-47

Those of us who have been forgiven much should love much. In other words, the amount of forgiveness that you and I embrace in our lives directly impacts the kind of love we will be willing to offer other people.

People like Simon the Pharisee have a problem with this message. Just ask current-day Pharisees. They feel like they have lived good lives and are solid people. They never sowed their wild oats or went on a drunken weekend bender. Unfortunately, since they have never fallen into these sins, they don't see why anybody else should either. This leads them to the mistaken idea that they don't need to be forgiven much.

But people who have struggled with sin typically show greater grace to fellow sinners. Like the woman in Luke's passage, they've been forgiven much, and this has empowered them to love much.

Discipline 10: Forgive those who are nearest and dearest

It happens to us all the time. We have been out on the road speaking for a week, two weeks, or even three, and we are feeling run-down, tired, and cranky. Such scenarios are fertile ground for fights to ignite, but we thank God that we have learned to live a life of forgiveness with those who are nearest and dearest to us.

"Lisa, I am so sorry that I put you through all of that," Al will say after a particularly grumpy drive between airports and hotels.

"Al, I hate so much that I put you through all of that grief," Lisa will say as she slips into bed after a day that went on too long.

Life is full of little frustrations and flare-ups, and if people aren't careful, these little issues can evolve into big-league problems. One person snaps at another, who snaps back, and then it's off to the races!

That's why we have worked on learning to forgive each other over and over, and why we remain committed to loving and forgiving each other rather than holding on to grudges and growing angry over time. When we hurt each other with little stings, we stop whatever we are doing and talk them out. That's how we keep these small daily issues from growing into major emotional problems. The question is simple: Are we going to hold on to it, or are we going to let it go? Letting it go wins every time.

The same principle goes for children who may have been hurt by your actions or words. We've tried to keep short accounts with our kids. And even though it can be embarrassing to confess your faults and failures to your own kids, they seem to embrace grace and forgiveness sooner and more easily than adults typically do. When our kids were young, a quick application of forgiveness helped our family get over the ups and downs of daily life together, and within minutes, the kids were usually back playing, having forgotten the latest of our silly mistakes.

Discipline 11: Forgive your political and ideological enemies
Jesus said to love your enemies. If He were here today, I believe He would make it clear that His command includes our political enemies.

Surveys and polls show that many Americans feel our national unity is being threatened by rising levels of hatred and violence. Public leaders don't merely criticize their opponents, but they also claim their opponents are enemies of the people or criminals who deserve long prison sentences.

Sure, it can feel good to demonize other people with whom you strongly disagree, but how can you do this without sinning against the men and women Jesus has commanded you to love? Remember His words in Matthew 5:43-45: "You have heard that it was said, 'You shall love your neighbor and hate your enemy.' But I say to you, Love your enemies and pray for those who persecute you, so that you may be sons of your Father who is in heaven."

God warned the Israelites about making idols, but it seems many Americans have made an idol out of politics. We get our opinions from angry commentators, not the Word of God. We allow our feelings about political issues to close our hearts to our neighbors for whom Christ died.

Being a good citizen is important, but we need to be careful that our powerful negative feelings about hot-button culture-war issues don't translate into powerful negative feelings for the people who disagree with us—people who desperately need Christ's forgiveness.

One year, Al's dad, Phil, was invited to speak at the Values Voter Summit, the big annual Washington, DC event for conservative Christian activists, organized by the Family Research Council. The *New York Times* had just published its explosive exposé on Harvey Weinstein, the Hollywood mogul who has since been accused of sexual abuse by more than eighty women. The #MeToo movement was off and running, and Dad was in typical form as he rose to speak.

"Hey, I suppose all of you have heard the latest newsflash," he said. "There is rampant sexual immorality in Hollywood!"

The crowd went wild, cheering and applauding. But then Phil threw them a curveball.

"But you know what? How are we going to help a guy like Weinstein? If we ever want to help people like this, we will have to forgive them."

Suddenly all the raucous cheers went silent. Deprived of more rhetorical red meat and reminded of their obligation to love their neighbor, everyone in the room was quiet.

Christianity was born into times that were as divisive as our day and age. Paul was imprisoned by Rome for spreading his faith throughout the empire, but Paul didn't use political power to gain his freedom. He sang hymns in his prison cell. When an earthquake rattled the jail and opened his cell door, he comforted the prison guard who had put him in stocks.

You may love the feeling you get when you're happily hating your enemies, but your hatred will never bring anyone to the love of Christ, and it will only make your own life miserable. Forgive your political and ideological enemies now, and continue to do so every time you feel the old hatreds flaring up again (and again, and again).

Discipline 12: Seek out sinners

We don't only need to love our political enemies. If we truly want to follow in the forgiving footsteps of Jesus, we must also seek out and love sinners who need forgiveness, desperate or otherwise. We shouldn't seek to quarantine ourselves from bad people but should rather reach out to them as ambassadors of God's loving-kindness.

Remember WWJD? This Christian movement asked an important question: What would Jesus do? One thing Jesus did a lot of was hanging around with sinners. As a result, the Gospels of Matthew, Mark, Luke, and John are overflowing with stories of desperate forgiveness. We've shared only a few of these stories with you in this book, but many of them show Jesus hanging out with prostitutes, tax collectors, and other "bad sorts."

How do you feel about desperate people? Jesus seemed to love them and get along with them just fine. That's the way we want to be too. We want to be around people who haven't yet come to love the Jesus we love, people who don't yet know what it means to be forgiven, people who haven't yet experienced relief from the many heavy burdens they carry.

We have a very practical way of putting out a big welcome mat for sinners at our church.

Our church has an active Celebrate Recovery program. If you haven't heard of Celebrate Recovery, the best way to explain it is to say it's a more explicitly Christian version of Alcoholics Anonymous. We host Celebrate Recovery meetings and programs for men and women dealing with all the problems that come from substance abuse and addiction. This attracts people to our church who some members consider "unsavory," but most members are fine with ministry to people with problems.

There is an interesting dynamic to recovery groups. Because members aren't allowed to have alcohol or drugs, they seem to overcompensate by consuming massive amounts of two other chemicals: caffeine and nicotine.

Some of our longtime church members didn't appreciate the sights or smells of people smoking cigarettes right outside the church doors and windows. So we came up with a compromise. We created a dedicated smoking section on the back side of our church. We've got a covered area where smokers can gather, rain or shine, and the area features a big butt dispenser for their finished cigarettes.

I (Al) make it my practice to visit the smoking area when I get to church. I always park in the back, and the smoking area is the first place I go. I hang out there with the guys and have a coffee with them as we talk. I don't smoke with them, but I always inhale plenty of their smoke, which fires up my allergy problems. And I believe that if Jesus were to come visit our church, that would be the first place He would go.

That's one way to hang around with sinners in need of forgiveness. What approach will you use?

Discipline 13: Pay forgiveness forward

Have you experienced the joy of forgiveness? Then help other people experience forgiveness for themselves.

Paying forgiveness forward is what we're doing with this book and our talks. But you don't need to write a book before you pay forgiveness forward. You can be a walking, talking agent of grace in your office, school, or neighborhood. Your job is not to pry into other people's business. Just keep your eyes, ears, and heart open for signs of sorrow and grief. When people share their burdens with you, offer them the healing balm of forgiveness. Help them find the same peace that you've found.

One great thing about forgiveness is that everyone can experience it. You don't have to be Christian or necessarily believe in any god. When an atheist gives or receives forgiveness, the feeling of relief can be just as significant and life-changing. Don't feel you need to convert someone to Christianity before they can experience forgiveness. In fact, we've seen many situations where an experience of forgiveness has been people's gateway to experiencing and embracing Christ's love for them.

You may even want to consider leading a Bible study or Sunday school class on forgiveness. It's an essential topic that doesn't get the attention it deserves. We've seen people give powerful teachings on why we need to both forgive and be forgiven. This simple lesson can be placed onto powerful Scriptures, such as the Lord's Prayer (Matthew 6:9-13) and the parable of the Prodigal Son (Luke 15:11-32).

You can also talk about your own experiences with forgiveness: how God has forgiven you for your sin, and how you have forgiven others for their transgressions.

Embrace the Gift

Christ died for our sins, paying the ultimate cost: His life. The apostle John's Revelation shows us that this sacrifice has led to Satan's defeat:

> And I heard a loud voice in heaven, saying, "Now the salvation and the power and the kingdom of our God and the authority of his Christ have come, for the accuser of our brothers has been thrown down, who accuses them day and night before our God. And they have conquered him by the blood of the Lamb and by the word of their testimony, for they loved not their lives even unto death."
>
> REVELATION 12:10-11

The desperate forgiveness you seek can be found if you embrace the forgiving blood of Jesus Christ, our Passover Lamb.

You no longer need to be bound by past hurts, habits, or hang-ups. This is the day your desperation can meet God's forgiveness! Don't wait any longer. Receive this valuable gift today.

Acknowledgments

We want to thank the many people who made this book possible.

First, we thank the brave men and women who allowed us to tell their stories of desperate forgiveness in this book.

Next, we want to thank the people at Focus on the Family who made it all possible. Thanks to Bob DeMoss, who invited us to bring our project to Focus. Steve Johnson helped us flesh out and focus our message. Julie Holmquist edited the final manuscript.

We also want to thank Steve and Lois Rabey for helping us transform our passion for forgiveness into the words you have read.

Notes

CHAPTER 1: DESPERATE FOR FORGIVENESS

1. "Not Ready to Make Nice," Martha Macguire, Natalie Maines, Emily Robison, and Dan Wilson, Kobalt Music Publishing, 2006.
2. Madison Gray and Tracy Samantha Schmidt, "The Amish School Shootings," *Time*, December 20, 2006, accessed December 6, 2018, http://content.time.com/time/specials/packages/article/0,28804,2011254 _2015215_2015212,00.html.
3. Dawn M. Turner, "Emanuel AME Church and the Audacity to Forgive," *Chicago Tribune*, September 28, 2015, accessed December 6, 2018, https://www.chicagotribune.com/news/columnists/ct-emanuel-church-charleston-dawn-turner-20150928-column.html.

CHAPTER 2: A FAMILY FORGED BY FORGIVENESS

1. Lee Habeeb, "Till Duck Do Us Part," *National Review*, August 20, 2013, accessed December 6, 2018, https://www.nationalreview.com/2013/08/till-duck-do-us-part-lee-habeeb/.
2. Ibid.
3. Ibid.
4. Ibid.

CHAPTER 3: THE WOMAN AT THE WELL

1. U.S. Department of Health & Human Services, Administration for Children and Families, Administration on Children, Youth and Families, Children's Bureau, "Child Maltreatment 2014," accessed January 7, 2019, http://www.acf.hhs.gov/programs/cb/research-data-technology/statistics-research/child-maltreatment.

CHAPTER 6: FORGIVENESS FOR THE DOUBLE-MINDED
1. Jesus Film Project, "Simon Peter: Portrait of an ENFP," November 2, 2017, accessed December 6, 2018, https://www.jesusfilm.org/blog-and-stories/simon-peter-enfp.html.

CHAPTER 7: PUT DOWN YOUR STONES
1. "Justice," Bruce Cockburn, Golden Mountain Music Corp., 1981.

CHAPTER 8: TALES OF THE FORGIVEN
1. Adapted from Joe Beam, *Getting Past Guilt* (Brentwood, TN: Howard Books, 2003), 117–121.
2. As told to Al and Lisa Robertson.

CHAPTER 9: CHOOSE FORGIVENESS, NOT DESPAIR
1. Centers for Disease Control and Prevention (CDC) WISQARS, "Leading Causes of Death Reports, 2016," accessed December 10, 2018, https://webappa.cdc.gov/sasweb/ncipc/leadcause.html.
2. Centers for Disease Control and Prevention, "Suicide Rising across the US," *Vital Signs*, June 7, 2018, accessed December 10, 2018, https://www.cdc.gov/vitalsigns/suicide/index.html.
3. Clay Routledge, "Suicides Have Increased. Is This an Existential Crisis?" *New York Times*, June 23, 2018, accessed December 10, 2018, https://www.nytimes.com/2018/06/23/opinion/sunday/suicide-rate-existential-crisis.html.
4. Ibid.
5. Lewis B. Smedes, "Is Suicide Unforgivable?" *Christianity Today*, July 10, 2000, accessed December 10, 2018, https://www.christianitytoday.com/ct/2000/july10/30.61.html.

CHAPTER 11: FORGIVING THE PRODIGALS
1. Jep and Jessica Robertson with Susy Flory, *The Good, the Bad, and the Grace of God: What Honesty and Pain Taught Us about Faith, Family, and Forgiveness* (New York: HarperCollins Publishing, 2015), 85.